Illustrated Guide to Hockey Sites & History
TORONTO

Steven Sandor

Vancouver • Victoria • Calgary

Heritage House Publishing Co. Ltd.
#108 – 17665 66A Avenue
Surrey, BC V3S 2A7
www.heritagehouse.ca

Heritage House Publishing Co. Ltd.
PO Box 468
Custer, WA
98240-0468

Library and Archives Canada Cataloguing in Publication
Sandor, Steven, 1971–
Illustrated guide to hockey sites & history : Toronto / Steven Sandor.

Includes bibliographical references.
ISBN 978-1-894974-19-6

1. Hockey—Ontario—Toronto—History—Guidebooks. 2. Historic buildings—Ontario—Toronto—Guidebooks. 3. Historic sites—Ontario—Toronto—Guidebooks. 4. Hockey—Ontario—Toronto—History—Miscellanea. I. Title.

GV848.4.C3S26 2007   796.96209713'541   C2007–901690–1

Library of Congress Control Number: 2006940150

Edited by Corina Skavberg
Proofread by Marial Shea
Cover design by Jacqui Thomas
Interior design by One Below
Front cover photograph supplied by the Hockey Hall of Fame

Printed in Canada

Heritage House acknowledges the financial support for its publishing program from the Government of Canada through the Book Publishing Industry Development Program (BPIDP), Canada Council for the Arts, and the province of British Columbia through the British Columbia Arts Council and the Book Publishing Tax Credit.

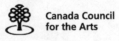

This book has been produced on 100% post-consumer recycled paper, processed chlorine free and printed with vegetable-based dyes.

Dedication

December 17, 1980: Toronto Maple Leafs 4, Minnesota North Stars 2.

In the stands: Karoly Sandor brings his son to his first NHL game. His nine-year-old boy will never forget that magical night.

Twenty-five years later, doctors diagnosed my dad with cancer, giving him at best a year to live. But no doctor counted on just how stubborn my father can be. So they called it a miracle when he beat cancer the first time around. His son knows better than to believe in miracles.

For you, dad. Keep fighting.

Contents

Acknowledgements

I would like to acknowledge those who have aided in my research for this book:

Susanne Willans and Barb Sisson
Toronto Granite Club

Lenard Kotylo
The Society of International Hockey Research

Kevin Shea and Danielle Siciliano
Hockey Hall of Fame

John Sewell
former mayor of Toronto

Geoff Wilson
Loblaw Companies Ltd.

Parker Neale
Toronto–St. Michael's Hockey Club

Rob Tunney
St. Michael's College School Arena

Dan Prendergast
St. Michael's College School

Les Duff
St. Michael's alumnus

Paul Babich
Balmy Beach Club

Introduction:
Toronto, A Hockey City

When it comes to sports, Toronto pretty well has it all. Canada's largest city boasts the Blue Jays, the country's sole surviving representative in Major League Baseball. Toronto is home to the Raptors, Canada's only remaining National Basketball Association club. The Argonauts give fans a chance to see Canadian Football on a regular basis. Meanwhile, the Buffalo Bills, a short drive around Lake Ontario on the Queen Elizabeth Way, is the city's de facto National Football League franchise. There's the National Lacrosse League's Toronto Rock who make championships an almost annual occurrence, and Toronto FC, a Major League Soccer franchise, is ready to kick off at Exhibition Place in 2007.

But regardless of how spoiled Toronto sports fans are when it comes to choice, make this clear. No matter how multicultural the city has become, no matter how much in-fluence America, just over an hour's drive away, has on this city, Toronto is and always will be a hockey town.

The Jays won the World Series in 1992 and '93; the Argos regularly make appearances in the Grey Cup; the Rock make championships look easy. But suffering Toronto fans would trade it all for the city's first Stanley Cup—or even a Stanley Cup final appearance—since 1967, when Punch Imlach's famous over-the-hill gang won the 13th Cup in the history of the Maple Leafs franchise.

Despite the Leafs' lack of success on the ice, there's no doubt that when it comes to attracting fans, the club is one of the most successful teams not only in hockey, but all of sport. It's about as easy to get a Leafs ticket as a seat at the Oscars. The season-ticket waiting list is so long, parents will place their newborn children on it in hopes that their kids will get the chance to spend thousands on tickets by the time they reach late middle age.

But Toronto is more than the Maple Leafs. The Greater Toronto Area is not only Canada's biggest megacity, but the biggest feeder of hockey talent to the professional game. A whole division's worth of junior hockey clubs play in the Greater Toronto Area.

Toronto is also home to the Hockey Hall of Fame, the permanent home of the Stanley Cup and all of the NHL's major trophies. It is the city that played host to the first Memorial Cup, emblematic of junior hockey supremacy.

While Montreal has won the most Stanley Cups and is recognized by the International Ice Hockey Federation as the official birthplace of the game (and there are still cries from Nova Scotia that it, not Montreal, is the true cradle of hockey) there is little doubt that the current world capital of the game is Toronto. For the people who live here, and for those who visit Canada's largest city, it is impossible not to notice how much of a role hockey plays in the daily lives of Torontonians. From the sports bars crammed with fans in Leafs jerseys to the community rinks packed with parents cheering on their kids, hockey is the key to the city's social fabric.

Whether you have lived in Toronto all your life or are just in the city for a weekend, this book will highlight the area's hockey history, from brand-new mega-arenas to small neighbourhood arenas and monuments.

The Leafs celebrate their Stanley Cup win with a parade in 1947. *Archives of Ontario 10011898*

The Granite Club:
Hockey's Golden Years

Today, the intersection of Church and Wellesley streets is famous as being the centre of Toronto's gay and lesbian community. But, this spot is also important as a landmark of Toronto hockey history. It was in the yards surrounding 519 Church, home of Toronto's best-known gay and lesbian community centre, that the city's first officially recorded hockey game occurred. It was also at this famous corner that the Toronto Granites, the first Canadian team to win ice hockey gold at an officially recognized Winter Olympics, was organized.

Photo of a decades-old team hangs at the new Granite Club, Bayview Ave. *N. Der*

Tracking an "official" first hockey game, whether it be the first in Toronto or the first in Canada, is an inexact science at best. The International Ice Hockey Federation officially recognizes Montreal as the birthplace of hockey, as the first recorded indoor game, with uniforms and rules, took place in that city's Victoria Rink back in 1875. But it will never be a claim that has 100 per cent backing of experts and historians.

Why? Because no sport is invented in one day. Hockey evolved over decades, possibly centuries. Nova Scotians claim that some form of hockey was played on outdoor ice in their province decades before the Montreal game, long before Canada was officially a country. There is no reason to doubt their claims, just as there is no reason to question the claims of New Englanders that there is strong evidence the game was also played in the Eastern United States in the 19th century, too. The true reason the world recognizes Montreal is because the Victoria Rink game, which featured a group of McGill University students, actually had a referee and a scoresheet.

The same rules apply when tracking the history of the game in Toronto. It's widely accepted that the first hockey game in the city's history took place on February 16, 1888, at the Granite Club, at the time the most famous and exclusive curling club in Toronto. The club converted its curling ice into a hockey rink for a special exhibition of the new sporting craze that was taking Eastern Canada by storm. The Granites and the rival Caledonia Club each gathered players, and the Granites claimed the game by a 4–1 score.

But to suggest that this game was the first time a Torontonian used a hockey stick to fire either a puck or a ball across a frozen sheet towards a net is silly. Of course there were variations of the game already being played in the city—just without official recognition, rules or a recognized league. In fact, hockey was likely played long before the 1888 Granites/Caledonia game. The 19th-century painter William Armstrong, famous for documenting life on the Great Lakes before Confederation, may have left a vital clue to hockey's origins in Toronto. In his painting "The Chief Justice Robinson landing passengers on the ice in Toronto Bay, 1852–53," which has a ship unloading passengers onto a frozen Toronto harbour in the foreground, there looks to be images of young boys playing hockey on a frozen patch.[1] Still, this can't take away from the Granite Club's honour as being the first "official" Toronto host of a hockey match.

There was actually quite a heated race between the Granite Club and the rival Caledonia Club to bring organized hockey to Toronto. In January of 1888, members of the Toronto Athletic Club and the Toronto Lacrosse Club were already selecting players to form a hockey team to send to an all-star tournament in Montreal, where the game had already taken root as the winter pastime of choice. Those clubs had entered into an agreement with the Caledonia Club to hold practices there.

Finding ice was a major challenge for the hockey teams. And it was a major concession for the Caledonia Club to agree to host the game. At the time, all the ice under arena roofs in the city was dedicated to curling. And curling requires a very different kind of pebbled ice than the fast, hard stuff used for hockey. So, the Caledonia Club decided to give up the ice only after some hard bargaining with the hockey players.

The 519 Church community centre as it looks today. *N. Der*

"So far, an arrangement has been arrived at by which the hockey players are to have the use of the Caledonia rink for an evening's practice, that it may be more clearly understood how much hockey playing will damage the ice for curling."[2]

Scouring the Toronto papers of the day for much news about hockey is a futile exercise; the sports write-ups of the time focus almost solely on curling. But this much can be deduced; interest in hockey grew so much at the Caledonia Club that the members decided to form their own team, but the Granite Club was more willing to sacrifice its ice. The crosstown rivals at the Granite had formed a team of their own, as well.

By February, the Granite and Caledonia clubs had taken over from the Toronto Athletic and Lacrosse clubs as the teams furthest along the curve when it came to embracing the new Canadian game of hockey—and it would be the Granite Club, which had more ice to spare thanks to a recent expansion, that added a second curling rink to its facility, sprawling across Toronto's northern boundary.

The Granites played their first game on their rink in 1888, but it would take another two years for the game to really hit its stride at that famous curling club. In February of 1890, the Rideau Rebels, a team that featured then-Governor General Lord Stanley's two sons, Arthur and Edward, took on the Granites. The Ottawa-based Rebels were arguably the game's most famous team outside of Montreal at the time, and the exhibition match was tipped as a real test for the fledgling hockey program at the Granite Club.

Not only was the game a test for the Granite's hockey skill, it was a test for their fists, as well. The brawl-filled affair saw fans rush onto the ice to join in the fray. The Rebels, as expected, won the game (by a narrow 5–4 score), but the brawls made headlines in the Toronto papers the next day.

Of course, Lord Stanley's sons helped fuel the Governor General's passion for the game and, in the same year the Rideaus made the trek from Ottawa to Toronto to play the Granites, he was part of the founding meeting of the Ontario Hockey Association. In 1892, he donated a small silver mug that became emblematic of Canada's hockey championship. The Stanley Cup remains one of the most famous trophies in sport to this day.

Thanks to exploding membership numbers and the fact that the city had grown and surrounded its site with urban sprawl, the Granite Club moved from its original Church and Wellesley site north to the corner of Yonge Street and St. Clair Avenue in 1925. Today, the club exists in a third location, on Toronto's wealthy Bayview Avenue.

But, before the club moved, the Church Street site still had one major hockey claim to fame—it served as the clubhouse for the famous Toronto Granites team that won Allan Cups, emblematic of Canadian senior amateur hockey supremacy, in 1922 and 1923. More importantly, the club represented and won gold for Canada at the 1924 Olympic Games in Chamonix, France.

Hockey was made part of the Summer Olympics program in 1920, and the Winnipeg Falcons won gold for Canada at the tournament. The success of hockey was one of the major reasons the Olympic movement wanted to add a winter program to its schedule. In 1924, known as the International Week of Winter Sport (for some strange reason, no one on the International Olympic Committee thought "Winter Olympics" was a fitting name for the event back then), the first Winter Games were held in France. Hockey officials in Canada decided that the

Historical plaque on the exterior of the old Granite Club building. *N. Der*

defending Allan Cup champs should represent Canada, so the Granites made the long steamship trip across the Atlantic to take on the best the world had to offer.

How good was that Granites team? Two forwards, Reginald "Hooley" Smith and Harry Watson, are enshrined in the Hockey Hall of Fame. After an illustrious amateur career with the Granites, Smith left for the National Hockey League. He would win a Stanley Cup with the Ottawa Senators, but gained more fame after he moved to the Montreal Maroons, where he played on the famous "S Line" with fellow legends Babe Siebert and Nels Stewart. But Smith wasn't the Granites' star player. That honour went to Newfoundland-born "Moose" Watson, who was named the most valuable player in Ontario senior amateur hockey in 1922 and '23.

According to Ted Reeve, the famed sportswriter for the *Telegram*, "The Granites could beat the Leafs on their lunch hour."[3] Of course, in 1924, the Granites would have faced the St. Pats, as the club hadn't changed its name to "Maple Leafs" yet, but Reeve was writing from an historical perspective.

No matter the NHL team, the Granites would have given them a game.

The Granites simply dominated the tournament. They played five games, and none were close. The Granites beat Great Britain 19–2 in their penultimate game of the tourney, and beat the United States 6–1 in the final. Watson scored the winner despite being knocked unconscious in the opening minutes of the game. It's not like Watson couldn't have scored in his sleep—he potted 37 markers in the five games. When the team returned to Canada, the NHL came calling and Watson stunned pretty well every hockey expert in the country by turning down the offers to play in the league, thus earning himself the title of the finest amateur player in history.

At the end of the tournament, the aggregate score for the five games Canada played in Chamonix was 110–3. It was a good thing the Granites were so impressive—their golden effort was the only medal Canada earned at the first Winter Olympics.

Team captain Dunc Munro did listen to the offers from the pros; he went to the NHL after the Games. He won a Stanley Cup with the Montreal Maroons in 1926, but his career was cut short by heart problems. Defender Bert "Mac" McCaffrey went on to play for the Pittsburgh Pirates and Montreal Canadiens; defender Beattie Ramsay left the Granites after the Olympics for Princeton University; he played hockey there and, after university, he skated with the Toronto Maple Leafs. Ironically, he would be the only member of the Granites gold-medal team to earn his way onto the hometown pro team's roster.

On the way home from Paris, the Granites team was feted in London, at British Columbia House. When the Granites returned to Toronto, the team was greeted with a massive parade and a special banquet held in their honour at the Granite Club on March 6, 1924. The menu's items were all named for or dedicated to members of the winning team. The fox salad featured Holy "Hooley" Dressing, and the cheese balls were described with a quote on the menu attributed to Ramsay, "High or Low, I love them so."[4]

There is no doubt that the site of the original Granite Rink is of large historical importance to Toronto. The modern Granite Club is now located in a well-to-do north-end neighbourhood on Bayview Avenue (and it's a members-only facility, so don't go there looking to snap photos uninvited), but it's the old site in the gay village that is of historical importance to the hockey fan. The modern Granite Club no longer has a hockey program. It's a member-driven organization, so any move to bring back the famous Granites name as either a junior or senior hockey program would require the club to vote for it to happen.

On an upper floor of the modern Bayview site, the skating rink can be found, home to a nationally renowned figure skating program. It is in a hallway across from the ice surface that the club's hockey memorabilia can be found. There's a photo of the Granite men getting ready to hit the ice, sticks in hand, from the winter of 1890. This team, featuring the likes of Joseph Walker, H.D. Warren Shanklin and Joseph Walker, would be the same one that took on Lord Stanley's Rideau Rebels. There's also a shot of Beattie in front of goal in the outdoor rink that was the centrepiece of Chamonix's Olympic site. Crowds can be seen around the rink, and hundreds more are watching the action from a mansion that had sightlines to the ice. The Alps are in the background, and Ramsay can be seen, wearing his simple "Canada" jersey, bearing down on the American goal in the final game of the tourney.

There is also a poster commemorating the Granites' 1922 Allan Cup win, with each and every member of the team pictured, including the star of the team, simply called "H.S. Watson" in the caption.

How to Get There

The site of the old Granite Club is now a community centre known as 519 Church. It's right at the corner of Church and Wellesley streets. Take the subway to Wellesley station and either walk one block east to Church or take the 94 Wellesley bus one block east. The 519 Church community centre is located on Church about a half-block north of Wellesley. It's on the east side of the street.

	Wellesley Subway	
Wellesley Street		site
College Street	Carlton	Street
Dundas Street		
Queen Street	Yonge	Church
King Street	Street	Street
Front Street		
Gardiner Expressway		

The Royal York:
Where Stanley Made the Rules

There's no arguing that the Royal York is Canada's most famous hotel. When it opened in 1929, the castle on Front Street was advertised as the most opulent hotel in all of the British Empire, let alone Canada. At 400 feet high, it was taller than any hotel in London. Over the years, it has hosted the who's who of celebrity, from leaders of states to rock stars to the royal family.

But, on the site on which it stands, another luxury hotel existed before the Royal York. The Queens Hotel, opened in 1862, was advertised as the finest hotel in the city; it would become a second home to many politicians who came to Toronto to debate the possibility of Canadian Confederation. It even hosted Confederate U.S. leader Jefferson Davis. It boasted capacity for 400 guests, still a large hotel by today's standards.

And, in 1890, it hosted one of its most famous guests, the Right Honourable Arthur Stanley, who would later become Lord Stanley of Preston. Stanley, who headed the famous barnstorming amateur Rideau Rebels club, the self-proclaimed best team in the country at the time, had fallen in love with this very new Canadian game of hockey. On November 27, 1890, he and several other hockey teams' managers gathered in a board room at the Queens Hotel to

The Royal York, just after it was completed in the late '20s, looms over Union Station. *Archives of Ontario 10002051*

discuss the future of the game. Why? Hockey games were being plagued with fights and disagreements over rules. Poor sportsmanship was more and more apparent in amateur games throughout Ontario.

Out of this hockey summit was formed the Ontario Hockey Association, comprised of 13 amateur teams, including Stanley's Rebels squad. It was in the Queens Hotel that hockey was transformed from a sport played in a poorly organized series of challenge games to being a recognized game with recognized rules played in the framework of a recognized league. It was a key moment in Canadian history, serving as a signpost for organized hockey in each and every province.

Hockey regulations had existed since the 1870s, when a group of McGill University students published rules. But the OHA executives, including Stanley, felt that these rules needed to be improved upon. The OHA standardized the number of players allowed on the ice (seven for each team, including a goaltender, two defenders, three forwards and a cover point), how long a game would be played (60 minutes divided into two 30-minutes halves) and the size of the goals.

Of course, as a modern fan can tell, the rules have undergone quite the overhaul since 1890!

The first OHA meeting was held in Toronto, but the league the trustees formed was dominated by Ottawa teams. One of the capital city's teams beat Toronto 5–0 in the championship game, winning the first OHA Championship, held in 1891.

Stanley was just getting started when it came to influencing what would become our great national game. Within three years, senior amateur teams from across the country would be vying to win the Dominion Hockey Challenge Cup, a trophy donated by Stanley that would be representative of a true Canadian hockey championship. That trophy is known to hockey fans around the world by its more famous name, the Stanley Cup.

As for the Queens Hotel, it stood until 1927; when Union Station, the city's major passenger rail terminal,

The Royal York today is still Toronto's No. 1 place to stay. *S. Sandor*

opened across Front Street, Torontonians pushed for a newer, larger and even more luxurious hotel to be built in the Queens Hotel's place. The Queens Hotel was demolished and replaced by the Royal York. After it was built, the

Royal York was one of the choice hotels for visiting National Hockey League clubs. And it was the headquarters of the Chicago Black Hawks in 1938, when they pulled off one of the greatest upsets in the history of the Stanley Cup.

It's hard to find a team that has inflicted more misery on Leafs fans than the boys from Chicago. The Hawks won the first-ever game at Maple Leaf Gardens; when the Gardens had its closing night in 1999, Chicago spoiled the party, hammering the Leafs by a 6–2 score. But those feats are nothing compared with what Chicago did to Toronto fans in 1938.

That season, the Hawks finished with just 14 wins in 48 games. But, thanks to the fact the Detroit Red Wings got just 12 wins, the Hawks clawed into the last playoff spot in the American Division. As fans know, once teams get into the playoffs, anything can happen. The Hawks won a couple of playoff rounds and ended up in the Cup final. But they would have to face the heavily favoured Leafs, champs of the Canadian Division, with 24 wins and nine ties in 48 games.

To make the odds all the more uneven, Hawks starter Mike Karakas was felled by a broken toe suffered in his team's semi-final clinching game. Because NHL teams carried just one goalie at the time, the Hawks tried to invoke an emergency clause that would allow them to bring a goalie from an already-eliminated NHL team into their roster until Karakas was healthy enough to play. When the Hawks arrived in Toronto and set up their makeshift headquarters at the Royal York, coach Bill Stewart decided that he wanted Rangers' goalie Dave Kerr as his emergency replacement.

The roadblock in the rulebook was that the opposing

team had to agree to the goaltender selected. And the Leafs, starved for a Cup, refused the Hawks the chance to get another NHL goaltender. The Leafs had consistently finished atop the league standings throughout the '30s, but had just the '32 Cup to show for their efforts. The Leafs did not want another playoff failure, so they vetoed Kerr.

The Hawks had to resort to a hunt for minor-leaguers. On the day of Game 1, the Hawks learned that minor-league journeyman Alfie "Half Pint" Moore might be available; he resided in Toronto during the off-season. Legend has it that Moore was found in a Toronto tavern on game day. But, the Hawks still tried to get Kerr into the series up until the face-off of Game 1 at the Gardens, when Stewart and Leafs owner Conn Smythe came to blows in a hallway.

As the Leafs had last say over who would play in goal, it was their general manager, Frank Selke, who informed Moore he would be playing. Basically, Moore was told to come to the rink, to bring his equipment and be ready to play. Moore would allow just one goal in Game 1, and spurred the Hawks to a Cup win. But, while Moore was happy to get his name on the Cup, he was bitter about being treated like a pawn in a battle between the Hawks and Leafs. Selke, in rebuttal, says he merely advised Moore to bring his gear to the Gardens on the off chance that he might be invited to play in a Stanley Cup final, "an outstanding honour, as Selke saw it, for any minor leaguer."[1]

The 1938 final was an especially bitter affair—and one to be remembered. Maybe, as you stand in the lobby of the Royal York, you can imagine the 1938 Black Hawks gathering, ready to leave for Maple Leaf Gardens, and pulling off one of the greatest David-versus-Goliath victories in North American sporting history.

How to Get There

Take the subway to Union Station. From there, walk up-stairs to the train station. The hotel is across the street. The construction of Union Station transformed Front Street, and was the major catalyst for the demolition of the old Queens Hotel. Go across Front Street to the Royal York Hotel. There is no trace left of the old Queens Hotel, but the Royal York gives you an idea that the north side of Front Street has always been the city's most famous address for visitors. It is now as it was over a century ago—the place for the rich and famous to stay when they come to Toronto.

The Balmy Beach Club:
Over 100 Years of Hockey

The Balmy Beach Club is one of Toronto's most famous sporting institutions, but hockey wouldn't be the first thing most members would think of when asked about the history of their organization. After all, the Balmy Beach Club's roots is as a canoe club, and the many national and international paddling championships—including Olympic medals—won by its members over the last century are testament to the excellence of the program. As well, Balmy Beach once boasted one of the finest amateur football teams in Canada. In fact, the Club has two Grey

The club logo, facing Balmy Beach. *N. Der*

Cup championships to its credit, 1927 and 1930, and some of the game's early great pioneers can trace their gridiron careers back to this club.

But hockey did play an important part in the Club; pictures on the walls of the lounge show "Balmy Beach Success" teams organized and playing hockey as early as 1906, just a year after the BBC was established right on the sands of Balmy Beach on the east end of Queen Street. It is proof that, after the curling clubs of the 19th century, Balmy Beach was one of the first athletic associations in Toronto to adopt hockey as a regular program sport, a mean feat considering that, since the club was founded in 1905, it has never featured a rink of its own.

Taking into consideration that the oldest athletic club in existence in the city—the Granite Club—discontinued its hockey program, you could argue that the Balmy Beach Club, which still runs a senior men's league at the nearby Ted Reeve Arena and also boasts an old-timers team, can boast the longest-running hockey tradition in the Greater Toronto Area.

The old-timers touring team has played in tournaments throughout the world, including games in the former Czechoslovakia, Poland, Italy and even Hungary. In 1987, the Balmy Beach Old Boys went to France to play professional second division teams from that country, winning two of three games played; the 7–6 victory over Cholet and 3–2 triumph over Toulouse are some of the greatest achievements in Old Boys history.

The Beach (as the neighbourhood is known now) where the club is found features a long stretch of sandy parkland that stretches just to the south of Queen Street East. It is now one of Toronto's most exclusive neigh-

On the walls, a link to a century of hockey tradition. *N. Der*

bourhoods, filled with expensive beach homes and pricey boutiques.

The club was founded in 1905, after authorities decided to protect Toronto's eastern beaches area from over-development and a railway line. Within years of the decision to save the beach, it became one of the city's places to be. Two years later, the area celebrated the opening of the Scarboro Beach Amusement Park, a boardwalk tourist attraction designed to make The Beaches of Toronto as famous as New York's Coney Island. The Scarboro Beach Amusement Park later failed in its bid to become Coney Island North; it was soon sold off to developers. But this didn't stop the area from growing.

The park split up Balmy and Kew Beaches, and helped create a rivalry. The Kew Beach Club soon had a hockey team of its own, and it would square off against the Balmy Beach Club after 1913 at a skating pavilion constructed at

Kew Beach Gardens just off Queen Street, a few blocks to the west of Balmy Beach Club. In 1917, Kew Beach won a Toronto senior men's league title thanks to the work of netminder George Hainsworth; the Hall of Fame goalie would go on to lead the Montreal Canadiens to two Stanley Cups. He would post 22 shutouts in a 44-game NHL regular season, still a record, and he would win the first-ever Vezina Trophy, which the NHL now annually awards to the league's top netminder.

The Balmy Beach team, coached by future CKEY Toronto radio personality Joe Crysdale, who became famous in Toronto for his work calling Maple Leafs baseball games from Christie Pits, won Toronto senior league titles in both 1949 and 1951. These championships were not noticed by the press at the time, who were more concerned with top-tier Ontario senior hockey, junior games and, of course, the Leafs, but those Balmy Beach clubs are notable.

Sports memorabilia crowds in the lounge of the Balmy Beach Club. *N. Der*

They featured two players who would go into the Balmy Beach Club's own Hall of Fame: "Iron" Joe McNulty and Tom Ford.

Ford was more famous as a football player; he is still considered one of the greatest halfbacks in Canadian football history and earned three Grey Cup titles.

George, his brother, also played hockey for the Balmy Beach Club; he graduated from that program just after the Second World War and caught on with the Barrie Flyers' junior team. With the Flyers, Ford played in the 1948 Memorial Cup final, which saw the Balmy Beach hero enjoy a homecoming of sorts, as the series would be contested at Maple Leaf Gardens. Like Tom, George is in the club's Hall of Fame. But despite their best efforts, George Ford and the Flyers were overmatched by the Port Arthur West End Bruins, who swept the series.

From there, George Ford went on to a lengthy pro hockey career in various North American minor leagues. But, like many other talented players of that era, Ford never got his shot at the National Hockey League. With only six teams at the time, spots were exceptionally limited.

Balmy Beach skaters didn't get a regular rink to play at until 1954 when, partially due to the fundraising efforts of the club, the Ted Reeve Arena was constructed on Main Street in East Toronto, a few blocks north of the club. To this day, a Balmy Beach Club senior men's league plays all of its games out of this facility. The arena is named for the football player and coach who founded Balmy Beach's famed football program. After a distinguished career on the gridiron, Reeve became one of the city's most famous sportswriters.

The Club survived fires in 1936 and '63; both blazes

totally razed the club, so the one you see today is actually the third building to bear the Balmy Beach Club logo on the front entrance. The area directly behind the club is public beach, so you can swing around and look at the beautiful mural painted on the back wall of the club, underneath the terrace, which faces Lake Ontario.

How to Get There

To get to the Balmy Beach Club, take the 501 Queen streetcar eastbound to Beech Avenue, just a couple of stops before the route's eastern terminus at Neville Park Loop. You will see the Club at the foot of Beech Avenue.

To see the Ted Reeve Arena, take the 506 Carlton streetcar east to the corner of Gerrard and Main Streets. Or, take the subway to Main Station and take the 64 Main South bus to Gerrard Street.

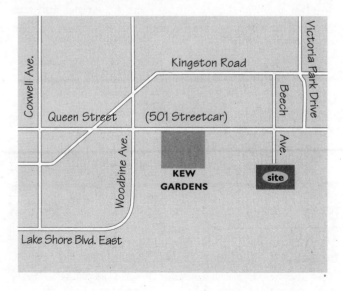

Arena Gardens:
Birthplace of the Leafs

If you look to the rafters of the Air Canada Centre, the current home of the Toronto Maple Leafs, you will find a banner commemorating the grand opening of hockey's new home in Hogtown, as well as a "Memories and Dreams" banner celebrating the nearly seven decades the franchise spent in Maple Leaf Gardens. But there is no banner celebrating the Leafs' first home. The franchise, first simply known as the Torontos, then the Arenas and later the St. Pats, was a charter member of the National Hockey

The Arena Gardens, the jewel of Mutual Street. *Hockey Hall of Fame*

League in 1917. Maple Leaf Gardens did not open until 1931. Unfortunately for many Toronto hockey fans, the team's formative years at the old Arena Gardens on Mutual Street are simply not remembered at all.

The Arena Gardens, a multi-purpose facility designed by the architectural firm of Ross and MacFarlane, with seating capacity for 8,000, was the key to Toronto finally becoming recognized as a hockey centre in Canada. When the Arena Gardens opened in 1912, the city had yet to win a Stanley Cup, simply because the city's teams could not get into the burgeoning elite circuits based in Eastern Ontario and Quebec. Without a major arena in Toronto, it wasn't worth the effort for the top teams of Ottawa, Montreal and Quebec City to make the long journey to the shores of Lake Ontario. Southern Ontario did have a pro "Trolley League" that existed a few years earlier, but it could not attract the calibre of talent that teams in Eastern Ontario, Quebec and Western Canada could.

But when the Arena opened, two Toronto clubs began play in the National Hockey Association, the forerunner to the National Hockey League, for the 1912–13 season.

The Torontos (unofficially nicknamed the "Blue Shirts" by the press because of the colour of their uniforms) kicked off a new era of pro hockey in Toronto on Christmas Day, 1912. A half-full arena watched the youthful Torontos actually take a one-goal lead into the third period against a veteran Montreal Canadiens squad. That lead could have been more than a goal if it wasn't for the play of future Hall of Famer Georges Vézina in the Montreal goal. The Canadiens' guile showed in the third, badly outscoring the Torontos in a game that ended in a 9–5 score. Don Smith led the way with four goals for the Canadiens. Still, the

Toronto's performance through the first two periods earned enthusiastic raves. "There were many in the crowd who came to look over the so-called 'lemons' which he (manager Bruce Ridpath) had gathered, but at the conclusion of the game they saw that the lemons had turned to 'peaches' and there and then became ardent supporters," read a sports column in *The Globe* on Boxing Day.[1]

Three days later, the Toronto Tecumsehs would kick off their NHA home schedule, also in front of about a half-full Arena Gardens crowd of 4,000. Like the Torontos, the Tecumsehs lost to a Montreal side. This time, it was the Wanderers who came out on the right side of a 7–4 score.

While the Torontos were somewhat successful in building a fan base, the Tecumsehs struggled. A season later, the Tecumsehs reorganized as the Ontarios. A year later, for the 1914–15 season, the Ontarios were reborn as the Shamrocks. Unlike Ottawa and Montreal, where hockey tickets were scarce, Toronto's interest in hockey as an alternative to curling and rugby was slow to grow. In the 1913–14 season, media reports of games between the Torontos and the Ontarios at the Arena Gardens indicated that they were poorly attended.

Even as the Arena Gardens hosted its first major final, Game 2 of the 1914 NHA Championship, advertisements ran in *The Globe* the morning of the game on March 11, 1914, advertising rush seats available for 50 cents each and re-served-seat tickets for a buck apiece. Obviously, the game was nowhere close to a sellout. Led by a hat trick from star Jack Walker, the Torontos whipped the Canadiens by a 6–0 score, giving them victory in the two-game, total-goals series.

At that time, the tradition was that the NHA champion accepted a challenge from the West's top pro team for

A housing co-op now stands at the 88 Mutual Street address. *S. Sandor*

the Stanley Cup. The Victoria Aristocrats travelled east to the Arena Gardens for the final, with Game 1 slated for March 14, 1914. The morning of that game, two problems faced the organizers of the series. The Cup trustees ruled that Victoria had not submitted the proper challenge paperwork to them, so if the Aristocrats won, they would not get the Cup. Basically, the Torontos had been forfeited the Cup before Game 1 even faced off. As well, advertisements ran in *The Globe* on game day advertising 1,700 rush seats available for the game at the Arena Gardens' box office. Judging by their lacklustre response, Toronto hockey fans smelled a rat.

Victoria planned to protest the trustees' ruling, so the series went ahead as planned. Toronto won Game 1 by a 5–2 count, the first part of what would be a three-game sweep. On March 19, 1914, Toronto would wrap up the series with a 2–1 win. There would be no hope for a protest, and the Arena Gardens, Toronto's home for hockey at 88 Mutual Street, hosted the city's first-ever Cup party, although, as poor ticket sales indicate, it was a muted one.

While the Torontos and their hardcore fans were agog with their quick march to success in the NHA, the neutrals were less impressed. Other leagues, such as the Ontario Hockey Association, played games in the Arena Gardens. Well-loved junior and amateur clubs such as St. Michael's, the Parkdale Canoe Club and the Toronto Canoe Club also played at the Gardens, and many observers considered the local brand of hockey superior to that of the pros. "It was the general verdict of the public that, as a hockey game, Saturday night's exhibition was 'punk,'" read a column in *The Globe* after Toronto's Game 1 win.[2]

Lord Stanley's Cup would make two more visits to the

Arena Gardens. The first came in 1918. The Toronto club, still without a name (the team was still known to the press as the Blue Shirts, but would eventually adopt the "Arenas" nickname for the 1918–19 season) won the championship of the brand-new National Hockey League, formed in 1917 thanks to then-Toronto club owner Ed Livingstone. How did Livingstone create the NHL, a deed not of his own choosing? The Hogtown hockey huckster merged the Torontos with the Shamrocks in 1915, and infuriated his fellow owners in the league by regularly trying to block the other NHA clubs from acquiring players. Livingstone was also all too vocal in his opposition of a 228th Battalion club, made up of enlisted hockey pros, being allowed into the league and playing out of the Arena Gardens during the First World War. By 1917, the majority of the NHA was tired of Livingstone. The other owners agreed to create a new league, the NHL, to replace the NHA—and Livingstone would not be allowed in. The Toronto club would be allowed in the new league as long as the ownership of the club didn't include Livingstone. The new Toronto club, run by Arena Gardens management, won the first NHL title, earning it the right to play the Pacific Coast Hockey Association champs from Vancouver in the 1918 final.

On March 30, 1918, Toronto star Corb Denneny decided a tense series by scoring the winner to give Toronto a 2–1 win in Game 5 of the five-game series at the Arena Gardens.

Four years later, the Cup would visit the Arena Gardens for the last time. The Arenas franchise, renamed the St. Pats for the 1919–20 season, won the NHL title, a surprise as the powerhouse Ottawa Senators were considered a shoo-in for the title. Like the 1918 final, Vancouver provided the opposition at the Arena Gardens. And, just like 1918, the series would go to a deciding, winner-take-all fifth game.

Had it not been an amazing two-sport athlete by the name of Cecil "Babe" Dye, maybe the Vancouverites would have taken the Cup back to the West with them. Dye was not only the hero of Toronto's 5–1 Game 5 victory over Vancouver, his nine goals in the 1922 five-game series led all scorers.

Dye almost didn't make it to the finals. He was due to report for baseball training camp by the time the Cup final rolled around, but the Buffalo Bisons (the minor-league baseball team for which Dye also starred) gave him special permission to stay with his hockey club. The Bisons' permission slip allowed Dye to put on the greatest individual performance in the history of the Arena Gardens. "To say that it was a triumph for the local right winger is putting it mildly," read the wrap of the game in *The Globe*.[3] "He dominated the attacking end of the play and he had the entire visiting team badly rattled as his rifle-fire shots went hurtling past."

The St. Pats still had a hard time getting a regular fan base, until 1927 when Conn Smythe, a First World War hero and noted hockey talent spotter, rounded up enough money for the $200,000 asking price for the franchise. Smythe desperately wanted an NHL team after he was dismissed from a general manager's post by the expansion New York Rangers the previous winter. He changed the team name to Maple Leafs—and through his unique mix of hockey passion and hucksterism, he turned half-full gates into sellout after sellout. The ticket-selling success of the Maple Leafs made Smythe realize that the team had outgrown its 8,000-seat rink. In 1931, the Leafs left Arena Gardens behind for their new Maple Leaf Gardens home just a few blocks north at the corner of Church and Carlton.

The Arena Gardens isn't only important as the site of Toronto's first Stanley Cup win; the arena also played host to the first Memorial Cup final, symbolic of Canada's junior hockey championship.

Named for the veterans who served in the First World War, the Memorial Cup was first contested at the Arena Gardens on March 19, 1919. The game was delayed because of parades honouring soldiers returning home from Europe—but when play did begin, the Regina Patricias were no match for the University of Toronto Schools team. U of T took Game 1 by a 14–3 count, and came back in Game 2 of the total-goals series with a 15–5 walloping of the boys from the prairies.

The local team had a massive home-ice advantage; U of T Schools used Arena Gardens as its de facto home rink for the season, as the school's own Varsity Arena was still six years away from being built.

In 1920, the Arena Gardens hosted the Memorial Cup final. Lionel Conacher, who would be named Canada's athlete of the half-century, played with the Canoe Club Paddlers squad that defeated a team from Selkirk, Manitoba. And, in 1921, the Gardens hosted one of the most exciting Memorial Cup finals in history. The Winnipeg Falcons trounced the Stratford Midgets by a 9–2 score in Game 1 of their two-game total-goals series. Of course, the Falcons believed the second game would be merely a formality. As in the 1919 U of T/Regina battle, one pummelling would be followed by another.

But Stratford, led by budding star Howie Morenz, would not let that happen. Winnipeg did end up taking the Memorial Cup, but not before the "Stratford Streak" and his Midgets mates put a hell of a scare in the Manitobans. With a 7–2 win in Game 2, Morenz and company showed heat and courage in almost pulling off a comeback. Morenz, a future Hall of Famer, would become one of the most-loved stars of the new National Hockey League, winning three Hart Trophies as Most Valuable Player before his tragic death in 1937 from an embolism suffered while recovering from a broken leg in hospital. Morenz's number 7 now hangs from the rafters of the Bell Centre in Montreal and he is regarded as one of the best-ever Habs in history. But it could be argued that Morenz's coming-out party came in Game 2 of that final at the Arena Gardens.

After the 1921 final, the Cup moved to Winnipeg, beginning its tradition of moving from Canadian city to city each year. But, for its first three glorious seasons, the Arena Gardens was the permanent home of the Memorial Cup.

After the championships, the Arena Gardens played host to another significant hockey moment. It was in a tiny, makeshift booth set up at the Gardens in 1923 that a young cub reporter by the name of Foster Hewitt first called a senior amateur game via telephone. Hewitt, of course, would become the famed voice of the Maple Leafs and the man who defined the radio and early television days of Hockey Night in Canada. Hewitt may have been famous for telling Conn Smythe to place the gondola at Maple Leaf Gardens, but it was at the Arena Gardens where he first called a game—and it had nothing to do with the Leafs.

There isn't much left of the old Arena Gardens. Its named was changed to the Mutual Street Arena after the Leafs moved out, and in 1962 it became a roller rink known as the Terrace. In 1989, the arena was razed, with very little protest, to make way for a housing co-op. For most Torontonians, the old Arena Gardens was an ugly child, not worth saving. Not worth saving the memories of Toronto's first Stanley Cup. Not worth saving the memories of the great junior teams that skated there.

The building also housed the first United Church rally in Toronto, and musical greats like Frank Sinatra and Glenn Miller played there. But the site is, first and foremost, a hockey rink.

The Site

In 1993, the Toronto Historical Board placed a plaque on an easement that you will find right next to the driveway leading into the Terrace Housing Co-Op. It's not right on the sidewalk, so it can be a little tough to spot. When walking south on Mutual Street from Dundas, you will come to the driveway for the Co-Op, which has the same 88 Mutual Street address as the old Arena Gardens. On your right, you will see a small square of evergreen plants, with a stone pillar behind them. It's on that stone pillar that you will find the plaque. When the wind blows just right, the evergreens obscure the pillar and plaque.

The historical significance of the sight is unfortunately lost on many of the people who now call the neighbourhood home. When the manager of the Co-Op was contacted, she said she knew that an old roller rink stood on the site, but said she was surprised—and quite thrilled—to find that her office was on the site of old Stanley Cup games and Memorial Cup championships.

Stand at that spot for a second and look at the old

THE ARENA GARDENS

ON THIS SITE, THE ARENA GARDENS, AT THE TIME CANADA'S LARGEST INDOOR FACILITY, OPENED 7 OCTOBER 1912. IT BECAME THE NEW HOME OF TORONTO'S FIRST PROFESSIONAL HOCKEY TEAM, THE TORONTO ARENAS, LATER RENAMED THE TORONTO MAPLE LEAFS. BESIDES HOCKEY, OTHER SPORTS, INCLUDING BICYCLE RACING, CURLING, BOXING, WRESTLING AND TENNIS USED THE SPACE. ON 20 JUNE 1925, THE BUILDING HELD THE INAUGURAL SERVICE OF THE UNITED CHURCH OF CANADA. REMODELLED TO INCLUDE ROLLER SKATING FACILITIES AND RENAMED THE MUTUAL STREET ARENA IN 1938, IT HOSTED THE GLENN MILLER BAND IN 1942 AND CROONER FRANK SINATRA IN 1949, AS WELL AS THE CITY'S FIRST BOAT SHOW IN 1954. THE ARENA WAS EXTENSIVELY REMODELLED IN 1962 AND RENAMED THE TERRACE. IT WAS DEMOLISHED IN 1989

TORONTO HISTORICAL BOARD, 1993

The historical plaque at the Arena Gardens site isn't easy to find. *S. Sandor*

Victorian homes across the street, the only buildings on the block that would have stood when the Leafs played in this neighbourhood. Imagine a street filled with hockey fans and the smell of popcorn. "On this site, the Arena Gardens, at the time Canada's largest indoor facility, opened 7 October 1912," reads the plaque.

Now close your eyes and listen for the slap of puck against stick, the cracking of steel blades as they carve the ice. Maybe for just a second you will actually feel the history of the place, that you are standing on the spot where a Toronto hockey team first hoisted the Stanley Cup.

How to Get There

The site of the Arena Gardens is now home to the Terrace Housing Co-Op, named for the arena that came before, located at 88 Mutual Street. The old arena faced Mutual

Street to the east and Dalhousie Street to the west. Dundas Street is to the north and Shuter Street to the south.

Is that all that is left of the place that cradled professional hockey in Toronto? Is that all that is left of the birthplace of the Toronto Maple Leafs?

To get there, take the subway to Dundas Station; from there, take the 505 Streetcar east to Church Street; get off and walk a block east to Mutual Street.

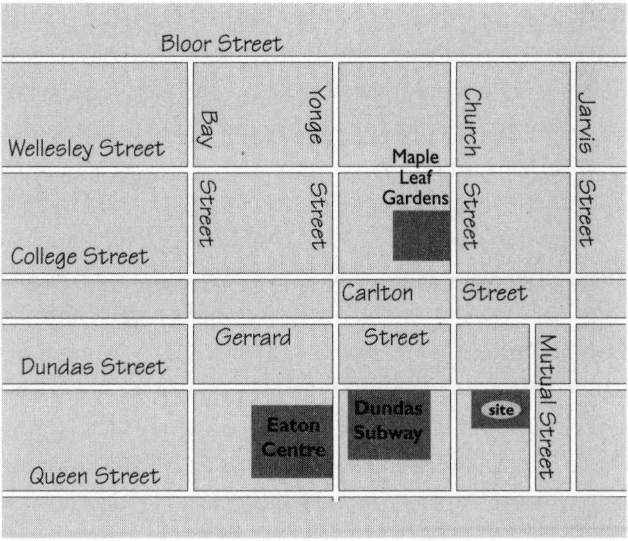

Bloor Street

Wellesley Street

Bay Street

Yonge Street

Maple Leaf Gardens

Church Street

Jarvis Street

College Street

Carlton Street

Gerrard Street

Dundas Street

Eaton Centre

Dundas Subway

site

Mutual Street

Queen Street

Ravina Gardens:
Home of the Rangers

When modern Torontonians think of the great buildings in their city that hosted National Hockey League teams, they're likely to name the Air Canada Centre and Maple Leaf Gardens. The odd one with a real penchant for history will name the Arena Gardens, the original home of the Leafs. But it would take a rare Toronto hockey aficionado to also name Ravina Gardens.

The building, located a couple of blocks north of High Park, was demolished in 1961, thanks to damage from groundwater in the ravine in which it was built. But, Ravina Gardens, built in the winter of 1925–26 on a park that was already a Toronto hotspot for outdoor hockey, was not only once the preferred practice facility of the Toronto Maple Leafs and the famous Toronto Marlboros junior club, it was also the rink in which the NHL's New York Rangers first hit the ice.

How can New York's famous Broadway Blueshirts trace their roots to a small park north of Bloor Street, in a field that now is little more than a place to hang out for kids on break at a public school just to the north?

In 1926, American tycoon George "Tex" Rickard, owner of Madison Square Gardens, was awarded an expansion NHL franchise. He named an emerging Toronto hockey mind by the name of Conn Smythe to be the general manager of the new club. Smythe had gained some notoriety in New York as he had taken a shorthanded University of Toronto squad to the Big Apple for some exhibition games against Ivy League schools, and he led the U of T to a series of impressive wins.

And, the new "Rangers" (Rickard wanted to name the team in the honour of famous lawmen, the Texas Rangers) would hold their inaugural training camp in the brand-new Ravina Gardens at 50 Rowland Street in Toronto's West Junction area, just a couple of blocks from High Park.

The park was already a popular spot for Toronto hockey by the First World War; an outdoor rink and a covered ice surface made it a prime spot for amateur teams and recreational leagues. The rink was also home to the Toronto Ravinas, a developmental squad under the wings of the NHL's Toronto St. Pats, later to become the Maple Leafs, in the early '20s. The popular Mercantile League, a fiercely competitive industrial league that featured teams from big

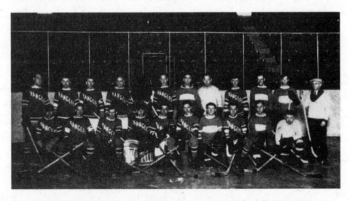

This extremely rare picture of the first Rangers team was taken in the fall of 1926 during the club's training camp at Ravina Gardens. *Hockey Hall of Fame*

Toronto plants such as CCM and Bunn's, also played at the rink.

However, the rink's use was limited to the coldest winter months, as the ice would begin to melt and play would be difficult by the middle of March in most years. So, a new "Ravina Gardens," with artificial ice, was erected to replace the old rink.

When the rink was completed, the Rangers became one of its first tenants.

The reasons for selecting Toronto as the site of the Rangers' training camp were fairly simple. Smythe was a Torontonian and pretty well the entire roster of players and camp invitees would be Canadians, so it would make sense to practice and do the dirty work of cuts on Canadian soil. As well, arena time was far more easily available in Toronto, where hockey was entrenched, rather than New York, where the game was a novelty and getting ice time to play hockey was difficult at best. Practicing in Toronto would be convenient to Smythe as the club could train on a regular schedule, and he wouldn't have to travel far to see the recruits in action.

That training camp was attended by some true hockey legends, including future Hall of Famers Bill Cook and Ivan "Ching" Johnson. But, despite the fact the Rangers had attracted plenty of star talent, not all was well during those early Ravina training sessions. Col. John S. Hammond, Rickard's right-hand man and president of Madison Square Garden, constantly clashed with the Rangers' general manager. While Smythe was negotiating a deal to bring star Frank Boucher from Boston to the Rangers, Hammond was also negotiating with the Bruins for the star forward, meddling in what had been agreed would be Smythe's job of negotiating deals and recruiting talent. The two soon butted heads. Smythe would not win the power play; before the team had left Toronto to begin the season in New York, Madison Square Garden fired Smythe.

If this kind of soap opera had occurred in the modern NHL, it would have made headlines across North America. But, hockey was such a novelty sport in New York at the time—the rival Americans had just begun play in the league one season before—it was not worth even a line or two's mention in the *New York Times*. But the news was of interest of the Toronto media, so the Rangers held a press conference to announce the move not in New York, but in Toronto's King Edward Hotel, which still functions as a downtown luxury hotel to this day.

On October 27, 1926, Hammond was successful in putting a positive spin on the Smythe mess. That day, Hammond introduced Lester Patrick, who coached the Victoria Cougars to the Stanley Cup in 1925 (the last non-NHL team to win the trophy), as the new boss of the club. Smythe was also on hand to smile and wave politely to the media. Smythe had to—the Rangers still owed him money.

Hammond told the Toronto media that the Rangers had decided that they needed a full-time hockey man to take over the club. When they first awarded Smythe a $7,500 salary (the amount Smythe had agreed to is actually the source of much debate; needless to say, money was another element to the Smythe/Hammond war), Hammond said the Rangers at the time felt that it was acceptable for their man to also focus time on his gravel business and treat hockey as a part-time passion. But, as training camp went on at Ravina, Hammond said the Rangers and Smythe agreed a full-time hockey man was needed, and Smythe had agreed to step down. Of course, this was a whitewash. In fact, Smythe had lost a bitter power struggle. But the press went for it, hook, line and sinker.

The show the Rangers put on in Toronto even fooled one of Canada's most famous sportswriters. Lou E. Marsh, for whom the annual trophy that goes to Canada's top athlete is named, wrote in his *Toronto Star* column the next day that all was well between Smythe and the Rangers. "Smythe and the Rangers part with the friendliest of feeling," Marsh wrote.[1] He also quoted Hammond as saying, "I am indeed sorry to lose Smythe. He has done exceptionally valuable work for us in putting together this team."

But, even though Smythe smiled for the press on that day, history shows us that he did so through gritted teeth. He had secretly vowed to get revenge on the Rangers, and that intention would be made public when he and a group of investors purchased the Toronto St. Pats, the NHL club that played out of the Arena Gardens on Mutual Street, in 1927. Smythe renamed the club, which shared the "Patrick" name of the man who had replaced him with the Rangers, the Maple Leafs and, in less than a half-decade, housed the club in the opulent Maple Leaf Gardens.

Had it not been for the charade at the King Eddy back on October 27, 1926, Smythe may have never got the emotional fuel he needed to buy the St. Pats; the team may have never changed its name, and Maple Leaf Gardens would never have come to be. That day at the King Eddy not only changed the fortunes of the Rangers, but of professional hockey in Toronto, as well.

How to Get There

Even though it's closer to High Park than Jane Street, the

only bus that runs down Annette Street leaves from Jane Station. Take the subway there and then transfer to the 26 Dupont Bus, which will head east down Annette Street. Get off at Clendenan Avenue. Annette Public School is on the south side of the street at the stop.

Or, if you don't mind a little walk, get off the subway at High Park station, then take the 30 Lambton bus north to Annette Street. Walk west to Clendenan Avenue. Walk south on Clendenan so you can get around to the back end of Annette Public School. Then, turn right until you get to a parking lot which leads onto a park right behind. You will notice how this small section of park space sinks below the street level. There's a couple of baseball diamonds and some old murals depicting Toronto of old painted onto the walls surrounding the park. They have been subject to years' worth of graffiti. Walk a little further and you will cross into another section of the park, with a playground and

A field is all that's left of Ravina Gardens. *N. Der*

wading pool. Imagine a time when this spot was filled with both an outdoor rink and an indoor "Gardens."

In 2001, the Toronto Historical Association recommended that Ravina Gardens be recognized as a lost historical site. Even though the building is gone, the THA felt that some recognition of the historical importance of Ravina Gardens should be placed on this site.

The King Edward Hotel

But, Rangers fans in Toronto should also visit the King Edward, the site of the famous sham the club sold to the press when Smythe was fired. The King Edward, now known as Le Royal Meridien King Edward, is located at 37 King Street East. To get there, take the subway to King station, then walk about a half-block east of Yonge Street on the south side of King.

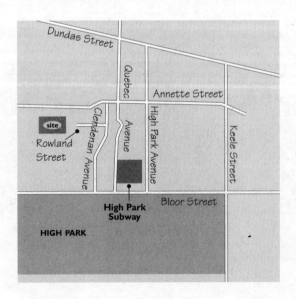

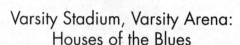

Varsity Stadium, Varsity Arena:
Houses of the Blues

It took a rally from students to get it built. There have been more than a few attempts to tear it down. But Varsity Arena, on the University of Toronto campus, continues to be the home to one of the finest collegiate hockey programs in Canada.

It has been more than two decades since the University of Toronto Varsity Blues have won a University Cup title, but its 10 titles stand second only to the University of Alberta as tops in intercollegiate history. The U of A may have surpassed the U of T as the top hockey school in the country, but a visit to the simple, functional 4,100-seat Varsity Arena reminds the visitor of the powerhouse Varsity Blues clubs and major title games that have been played here.

The Arena was completed in 1926, 34 years after the University of Toronto began sending teams to play competitive games in the Ontario Hockey Association. And it was only built after money was raised by students after years of public protest. After failing a building inspection, it was nearly razed in 1981, until an 11th-hour fundraising campaign and lottery grant saved the building. And, in 1999, the Varsity Arena once again escaped the wrecker's ball when the school decided that a planned project that would have seen the ice rink located under a new Varsity Stadium was not feasible.

For decades, Varsity Arena stood right next to the old Varsity Stadium, which was torn down in 2002. The U of T is rebuilding the facility. And it's at this old Varsity Stadium site where the earliest days of campus hockey can be traced.

The University of Toronto's own website[1] states that school-based hockey teams played at the old Victoria Curling Rink on campus at 277 Huron Street, a brick Victorian building designed by Norman Bethune Dick. Dick was a member of the Granite Club—the same Granite Club that hosted the first recorded hockey game in Toronto history in 1888. The Victoria Rink was finished the year before the Granite began hosting hockey. Like the Granite, the ice for the Victoria Rink was designed for

A University of Toronto women's hockey team, circa 1912. *City of Toronto Archivess, fonds 1244, item 480*

curling, and was not optimal for hockey. The experiment to play hockey in that facility was short-lived. The biggest hockey moment for the old Victoria Rink came in 1899, when it hosted the Ontario Hockey Association finals between the U of T and Queen's University, which the team from Kingston won.

For the most part, the U of T played outdoors or at the Caledonia Club's curling rink on Mutual Street, which would later be torn down to make way for the Arena Gardens, when it first iced a varsity team in the Ontario Hockey Association in 1892. In 1903, the Varsity Blues team joined the Intercollegiate League, made up of schools in Quebec and Ontario—and quickly asserted itself as not only a university hockey power, but possibly the best amateur hockey program in Canada. For sure, the team was the top hockey program of any sort in Toronto at the time.

By 1908, the Blues were easily in the class of university hockey. Led by scoring star Herb Clarke, the team came into the 1908 season as defending intercollegiate champs. To say that the team was dominant would be an understatement. The Blues would often hit double digits in goals scored in their league games. The team clinched the championship over Laval, at the time considered the Blues' top rival for the title, with a comprehensive 9–0 win. The team's season included a 15–5 win over Queen's and a 19–1 win over Laval. That's right—19–1! "It seems like boasting to say that there is not an amateur team around to beat Varsity, but somebody has to say it..." wrote R.Y. Cory, sports editor of the campus organ, *The Varsity*.[2]

Despite the U of T's fame as a hockey school, the team was reduced to playing its home games either on a frozen sheet on the varsity fields, or the team would travel to the Mutual Street rink that predated the Arena Gardens. (The spot on which the varsity fields lay would be where the original Varsity Stadium was built, and it would later be rebuilt into a nearly 20,000 seat stadium in 1924.) The Mutual Street facility, designed for curling, not hockey, and located away from the campus, was the best facility in the city at the time, but had a smaller-than-regulation ice surface and paled in comparison to the facilities used by other university teams in the Intercollegiate League.

U of T games were often plagued by snow or slushy ice, and visiting teams and U of T supporters complained loudly about the sad state of affairs. Hockey was booming in popularity. Before 1908, two rinks were created on the surface of Varsity Stadium during the winters, and that year, thanks to the rising number of players and intramural teams on the campus, that number was increased to three. To make the three rinks fit on the Varsity fields, each ice surface was made smaller than regulation, leading to even more cramped playing conditions. "It's a very strange thing indeed that a city of Toronto's size does not contain a proper rink. There is hardly a town in Ontario that has a better one than the Mutual Street, which is moreover very overcrowded."[3]

The Jennings Cup, contested between the various colleges on the U of T campus, was hosted mainly on one of the varsity surfaces, much to the disdain of players and fans alike.

Things got a little better for the hockey program in 1912, when the Arena Gardens, at the time the largest indoor arena of its kind in Canada, opened on the site of the old outdoor rink on Mutual Street. The Varsity Blues moved into the brand-new rink, but the arrangement was far from perfect. The Arena Gardens hosted two teams in the new

National Hockey Association, and the pro teams got the prime ice dates. Between pro games, amateur match-ups and a slew of other non-hockey events slated for the Arena Gardens, ice time wasn't easy to get. And, students complained that it was inappropriate for the Varsity Blues to be playing their "home" games so far off campus.

It was in this period that a hardworking forward emerged as a University of Toronto star. Conn Smythe's playing career would be cut short when he was sent to Europe to fight in the First World War, but not before he captained the U of T to a provincial title in 1915 with a win over the Berlin Union Jacks.

Students and fans would not mind making the pilgrimage to Arena Gardens in the 1918–19 season to watch the University of Toronto Schools team, a high school prep-school administered by the University. The club was built by Frank Selke, who would later go on to be one of the most hallowed general managers in NHL history, an architect of championship teams in Toronto and Montreal. In 1918, Frank Carroll took over as coach from Selke.

Frank Sullivan was the team's scoring star, while Dunc Munro, who would win Olympic gold in 1924 with the Toronto Granites, was the star defenceman. Despite winning the prep-school junior title in 1919, U of T almost forfeited the season when Sullivan was discovered to be too old to play. But, in the spirit of sportsmanship and in recognition of the fact the U of T had the best shot at a provincial title, the other Ontario prep-school clubs, which included Toronto's St. Michael's College, agreed to allow U of T to play challenge games without Sullivan in the lineup in a bid to reclaim their crown. Carroll's boys did just that and entered the Ontario playdowns.

The most thrilling game of the playdowns saw the U of T take on the famous Toronto Aura Lee Club, led by the legendary future Hall of Famer Lionel Conacher. "The team was packed and, in fact, its manager had tried to recruit Dunc Munro from UTS (University of Toronto Schools). If you switch teams, Aura Lee's manager promised Munro, I'll get you a place in school at Upper Canada College."[4]

More than 7,000 fans packed the Arena Gardens to see the game. After shooting off to an early 7–3 lead, the Blues held on for a 7–6 win. After beating Woodstock and Quebec's Loyola College in further rounds, the U of T qualified for the first-ever Memorial Cup final—Canada's new national junior championship. The Blues overwhelmed the Pats at the Arena Gardens, taking two games by an aggregate 29–8 score. If anything, the Blues' later-round and final games proved that Aura Lee was really the second-best junior club in the country, not Regina.

Ironically, after complaints from university-age students that the UTS high schoolers were taking up too much time on campus outdoor rinks, UTS moved into a shared practice space with Aura Lee at Avenue and Davenport Roads after winning the Memorial Cup.

In 1920, university students, tired of not having a proper rink on campus, began a fundraising campaign to get a proper arena built. Cost estimates for a 7,000-seat rink came in at $400,000. A year later, bonds ranging in price from $100 to $150 were put on sale to the general public in an effort to get the arena project funded. Those who bought shares would be guaranteed tickets for games at the new arena. Remember that Maple Leaf Gardens was still a decade away from the drawing board. Obviously,

Centre ice at the Varsity Arena. *University of Toronto*

there were hopes that an opulent arena at the U of T would rival the Arena Gardens on Mutual Street as the top facility not only in the city, but the country as well. Their efforts were spurred by the success of the Blues, which took the Allan Cup as Canada's national senior champions in 1921.

But the $400,000 7,000-seat arena was too ambitious a plan to be realized. By the time construction was completed in 1926, the project was scaled back to $275,000 and just over 4,800 seats. The Varsity Arena was designed by U of T professor Tommy Loudon, who also doubled as the school's rowing coach. Loudon had also designed the new stands in the Varsity Stadium renovation of 1924.

The new Arena would accommodate one hell of a hockey program. At that time, no collegiate program anywhere in North America could boast of a team as good and as consistent as the Varsity Blues.

When he returned from the war, Conn Smythe turned his attention to his fledgling gravel business and his passion—hockey. He took over as coach of the Varsity Blues in 1923, two years after the team captured the Allan Cup as Canada's senior amateur champions. The Blues would win intercollegiate title after intercollegiate title under Smythe, who remained on as coach until 1926, when the New York Rangers hired him to become the general manager of that new franchise—a job that would last only a few weeks until Smythe was forced to resign. From there, Smythe would buy the Toronto St. Pats and transform them into the Maple Leafs.

In 1925, Smythe coached the U of T to the Allan Cup final, but the Blues came up short against the opposition from Port Arthur. That set the stage for an epic rematch at the Arena Gardens in the 1926 final. Varsity Arena was not yet complete, so this would be the last major final the Blues of this generation would have to play off-campus. The 1926 final is still regarded as the finest Allan Cup ever played. The deciding game was tied 3–3 after referees called the game when three overtime periods were completed. The make-up game finished 2–2 and had to go to overtime. It was in this second overtime that Port Arthur finally got the winner, devastating the home team and its fans.

The Blues did get some consolation when they travelled to New York and thrashed Ivy League champions Dartmouth by a 6–1 score. It was this effort that attracted Madison Square execs to Smythe's abilities as a manager and coach.

The Blues were so bitter at their Allan Cup defeat, and buoyed by their success in New York, that they decided to stick together, even though many of the players were graduating from the school.

The Grads would usurp the Varsity Blues as the new Varsity Arena's prime-time tenants. The Arena opened on December 17, 1926, with the Blues taking on the Grads in a two-period exhibition game. The Grads won 3–0.

That season, after Smythe left the U of T program, the Blues would be coached by future Canadian prime minister Lester B. Pearson, who led them to two league titles in his two seasons behind the bench.

As the Blues kept winning, the Grads, with Smythe behind the bench again after being forced to resign by the Rangers, were out to avenge the Allan Cup losses of 1925 and 1926. They would win the Eastern Canada playdowns as they had the previous two seasons, and earn the right to play the Fort William Thundering Herd in the finals. The all-Ontario final would be held in Vancouver, of all places.

Neither team could boast home-ice advantage so far from home, but the U of T won the series in four games after a 2–1 overtime victory in the decider.

As the reigning senior men's champs at the time of the 1928 Winter Olympics, these Grads, the team that Smythe built, would become Team Canada at the Games. The Grads were allowed to skip the round robin of the hockey tourney at St. Moritz, Switzerland. In the medal round, the team went undefeated, winning three games by an aggregate score of 38–0 and capturing Canada's only gold medal of the 1928 Games. Hugh Plaxton and Dave Trottier each scored 12 times in the Grads' three wins.

Over the next four decades, no school could truly challenge the U of T's claim as the top hockey school in the country. The Blues continued to win league titles, and Varsity Arena remained the king of all university rinks in Canada. But, at that time, there was no formal coast-to-coast interuniversity hockey championship. But, when Canadian universities created the University Cup competition for the 1962–63 season, the nation finally had a true national intercollegiate championship. In 1966, the Blues won their first title under coach Tom Watt, who would later go on to coach the Winnipeg Jets, Vancouver Canucks and Toronto Maple Leafs. It would be the first of many. From 1966 to 1984, the U of T won 10 University Cup championships, including 5 in a row from '69–'73. Watt led the team to 9 of those titles, while the 1984 championship squad was coached by Mike Keenan, the same famous "Iron Mike" who would lead the New York Rangers to the 1994 Stanley Cup. So, between Smythe and Keenan, there is no shaking the strong link between the Broadway Blueshirts and the Varsity Blues.

When U of T won its first title, it left little doubt that there was still a wide gulf between it and other Canadian schools when it came to hockey excellence. In the '66 final series, the Blues drubbed Alberta 8–1, then in '67 destroyed Laurentian 16–2.

During that five-titles-in-a-row reign, Watt and the Blues hosted a team of Soviet university players in 1972, the same year Canadian NHLers took on the Soviets in the famed Summit Series. Like the Summit Series, the Canadians came out on top in the Varsity Arena game, but in not such a dramatic fashion. The Blues easily won the game by a 5–1 count, with John Wright going down in history as the player of the game with a hat trick. Wright would go on to play four NHL seasons with the Vancouver Canucks, St. Louis Blues and Kansas City Scouts.

The Arena would also host one pro season of hockey. When John Bassett, after being deposed from the ownership group of the Toronto Maple Leafs, needed a home for his World Hockey Association Toronto Toros, he chose Varsity Arena. The Toros played one season on the U of T campus before Bassett struck a deal to move the Toros to the Gardens. That move was a colossal mistake. Higher Gardens rent and poor crowds forced Bassett to move the Toros to Birmingham, Alabama, where they became known as the Bulls, and survived until the WHA itself folded in 1979.

Varsity Arena has hosted nine University Cup championship games, the most recent in 1992 when the University of Alberta Golden Bears won the title. Despite all of the final games it hosted, and the U of T's championships, only twice, in 1973 and 1976, did the Blues capture the University Cup on home ice. Believe it or not, the Blues' chief crosstown hockey rival, York University, has won more championships ('85, '88 and '89) on Varsity ice than the U of T.

A half-full Varsity crowd took in the '85 final, with York's Don McLaren, who also scored the winning goal at the '84 Spengler Cup, giving his school all the offence it needed with a hat trick in a 3–2 win over the University of Alberta. The U of A came back from a 3–0 deficit to beat the U of T in the '85 semifinal; had that comeback not occurred, Varsity would have been home to an all-Toronto University Cup final.

When the Canadian Interuniversity Athletic Union (CIAU) changed the format of the finals to a four-team "Nationals" tournament in 1988, Varsity Arena was chosen as the place where it would happen.

Those York teams were backstopped by Yeomen goalie Mark Applewhaite, who is now enshrined in his school's athletic Hall of Fame. While Applewhaite never went on to a significant pro career, he starred on Varsity Arena ice for all three York titles. He was named a tourney All-Star in all three championship seasons and bagged the title as MVP of the University Cup in 1989.

Varsity Arena has also played host to the U of T Cross/Border Hockey Challenge, which has pitted top Canadian and American school teams against each other, rekindling the spirit of the '20s, when Smythe took his U of T squad to America to face the Ivy League's best.

Varsity Arena and the University of Toronto also have a strong connection to women's hockey. In 1922, four years before the opening of Varsity Arena, the U of T and a group of players from McGill played in the first official women's intercollegiate game in history. But evidence points to the fact that women were strongly involved in hockey long before that on the U of T campus, playing on the outdoor winter rinks placed on the Varsity Stadium playing fields or on an outdoor rink near Burwash Hall on Charles Street, a few blocks west on the old Victoria College grounds. Photos dated as early as 1910 in the files of the City of Toronto Archives show women playing on this site.

On February 28, 1999, one season after Canadian universities created a national women's hockey championship, the women's final was held at Varsity Arena. While the U of T itself wasn't involved in the final, the game was notable, with the underdog Concordia University Stingers riding a hot goalie to upset the favoured University of Alberta Pandas. Goalie Jessika Audet turned back all 15 shots she faced and was named the game's MVP. Two years later, the Lady Blues would win a national title, in Calgary.

Even though the Varsity Arena continues to host major university hockey events, as well as student exams and ceremonies, it lives on borrowed time. Over the last three decades, the Arena has continually dodged the wreckers' ball. In 1977, Varsity Arena was deemed unsafe by the Toronto Fire Department. The Georgian-style brick building did not have the appropriate fire exits, and a new roof was needed. An exception was made for Blues hockey games, and the Arena remained in operation, albeit with a death warrant on its head. Four years later, the University began entertaining the idea of tearing the old arena down. Alumnus Hamilton Cassels championed a fundraising drive to save the arena, but it was in such bad shape, millions were needed. Cassels' drive managed to raise $400,000, not nearly enough to save the building. The Government of Ontario stepped in, and made $1.45 million in Lottario funds available for the restoration of the arena. By 1986, the Arena renovation was done. Capacity was reduced to 4,100, and the size of the ice surface was expanded to within just a few feet shy of NHL regulation size.

But, as the university continued to grow—and as neighbouring Varsity Stadium fell into disrepair—another plan was launched that would have seen Varsity Stadium and Arena replaced with a stadium that would have featured a hockey arena underground. While Varsity Stadium was not spared the wrecker's ball, the Arena survived. In 1999, a feasibility study suggested that the U of T would be better served if the new stadium project was scaled down to allow more room for new student housing.

So, thanks to the passion U of T students had for hockey, Varsity Arena was built. And, partly due to fundraising efforts and partisan efforts from the student body to save the old building, it still survives today.

But you still can't escape the feeling that Toronto's House of Blues won't be with us for very much longer.

Need Tickets?

Seeing U of T Varsity Blues hockey, whether it be the men or the women, is easy. Games are never sold out, so it's easy to stroll up to the Varsity Arena box office the day of the game and get a ticket. As of the 2006–07 season, tickets remained one of the best hockey bargains in the city. Adult seats are just $8, while students get in for $5 and children aged 5–12 can get $3 tickets.

How to Get There

Varsity Arena is easy to access from the St. George subway stop. At 275 Bloor Street W, it's located just outside the station. Use the St. George Street exit.

As well, the old Victoria Rink is now the Faculty of Architecture, Landscape and Design. It's a decent walk from the Varsity Arena, at the corner of College and Huron Streets. To get there from Varsity Arena, walk south down St. George Street until you get to College Street. Turn west on College and walk a block to Huron. Or, take the subway to Spadina and get on the connecting 510 streetcar going south. Get off at College Street and head a block east to Huron.

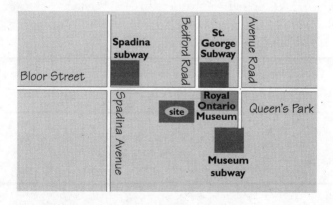

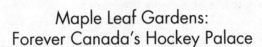

Maple Leaf Gardens:
Forever Canada's Hockey Palace

When you get off the subway at College Station, the ghosts of Saturday nights past can still be felt. The station features Montreal Canadiens players painted on the northbound platform, while Leafs players are painted on the southbound side. They face each other from across the tracks, poised for battle. Charles Pachter's "Hockey Knights in Canada," was placed on the walls of College Station when it was renovated in 1985.

The famous front façade of Maple Leaf Gardens, facing Carlton Street. *Hockey Hall of Fame*

The station is filled with photos of great Leafs past. Walk up the steps toward the surface, and you will pass photos of "King" Clancy, Darryl Sittler, Borje Salming, Wendel Clark, Doug Gilmour and Felix Potvin, to name a few. The exit signs still indicate which stairs lead out in the direction of Maple Leaf Gardens, as if thousands of fans are still expected to come streaming out of the trains minutes before puck drop.

But the building itself is a different matter. Many of the art deco font letters have fallen off the famous marquee that faces Carlton Street. The entrance to the old Hot Stove Lounge facing Church Street has been boarded up. Maple Leaf Gardens gives off the feel of a building that has been abandoned for decades, not years.

The exterior of the yellow-grey brick building is protected as a historical site, but the owners of the building are free to do with the inside as they please. There is no law

Murals in an entranceway celebrate the Leafs' past glories. Will anyone ever see them again?
S. Sandor

The famous Gardens marquee is in disrepair in 2006. *S. Sandor*

in place to prevent the removal and demolition of sections of seats or the destruction of the ice rink to make way for another use.

Still, even with the building in less-than-ideal shape, there is no shaking the magic at the corner of Church and Carlton Streets. Like many kids who grew up in the Toronto area, I can recall the first time I ever saw the Maple Leafs skate on the ice at the Gardens. A ticket to a Leafs game was a special treat, one that did not come easy. I was nine years old when my dad came home from work with a couple of tickets in hand. Now, a Leafs/Minnesota North Stars game may not have the same resonance as a Leafs/Canadiens game, but, for a young hockey fan who felt lucky when his parents would let him stay up to watch two periods of the Wednesday Leafs game on Channel 11, and who fought fatigue to make it through all three periods of *Hockey Night in Canada* on a Saturday night, those two tickets took on the same importance as Game 7 of a Stanley Cup final.

I can still recall more about that Leafs/North Stars game than many of the thousands of hockey games, from junior hockey to the Edmonton Oilers beat, from Stanley Cup finals to the World Cup of Hockey, I have covered as an adult. I remember Dan Maloney scoring the winner past a teenaged rookie by the name of Don Beaupre. And Darryl Sittler, more famous for scoring goals, got in a fight.

While the Gardens is recognized as Canada's hockey palace, it isn't an example of stupendous art deco design. In fact, Maple Leaf Gardens may go down as the most utilitarian project of its kind in Canadian history. "The Gardens is not the first enclosed arena, nor is it constructed of the 'finest' materials nor perhaps is the best work of the architects involved, nor is it an example of the purity of any particular school of design, but we find that it is an artistic and powerful, yet economic and humane expression of its program and purpose," read a 1990 report from the Province of Ontario recommending the historical designation, a move which the Maple Leafs themselves opposed.[1] "It is the 'core' building to a central and unifying animation of Canadian culture over a significant period of time."

In fact, Harold Ballard, the reviled Leafs owner who, two decades before, won a power struggle with the Smythe family and Toronto millionaire John Bassett to win control of the Leafs, was so incensed by city hall's efforts to have the Gardens designated a historical site, he told the Toronto Star that he felt then-mayor Art Eggleton and his city council were "Communists."[2]

The Gardens was built out of necessity. Conn Smythe,

who had bought the old Toronto St. Pats and renamed them the Maple Leafs in 1927, had turned hockey from a pastime that was played in front of a half-full Arena Gardens into a must-see event that would sell out the 8,000 seats. And even though Smythe's Maple Leafs packed them in, the team was losing money simply because the old Arena Gardens on Mutual Street didn't have the seating capacity needed to turn a profit. Smythe's argument for a new rink was really no different than the one the Leafs made for leaving Maple Leaf Gardens in 1999 for the Air Canada Centre. Modern hockey business people will use fancy terms like "creating new revenue streams" and "maximizing revenue," but it's a simple formula. More seats = more tickets for sale = more tickets sold = more money to be made.

But Smythe wasn't a rich man. Even though he had a successful gravel business, he was better known as a First World War hero and a prime spotter of hockey talent. Those are the credentials that could get a man fame, but not a massive paycheque. His $200,000 deal to buy the St. Pats was done thanks to the fact that new friend and St. Pats shareholder J.P. Bickell decided to leave his money in the club. When the search for a new arena began, Bickell and Sir John Aird, president of the Canadian Imperial Bank of Commerce, were indispensable allies, as was Frank Selke, Smythe's right-hand man who helped build the Leafs into a contender for the NHL title, but who never forgot his roots as a tradesperson and union brother.

Smythe had to sell the idea of a new Maple Leaf Gardens, as he did not have the money to build it himself. He solicited his rich allies for funds and, when that wasn't enough, he sent out flyers to the ticket-buying public encouraging them to buy shares in the building project.

Those flyers should still be required reading for any would-be advertising executive. Using a mixture of cartoons and rhetoric, Smythe outlined his need for a new arena in these

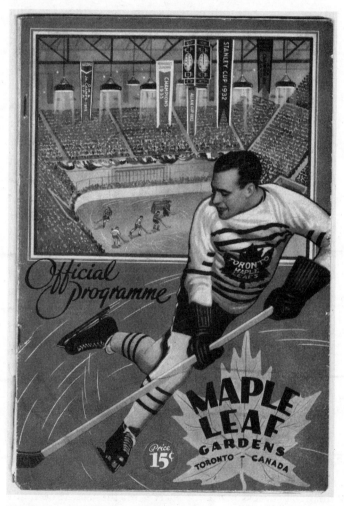

A Maple Leafs game program from the 1930s. *Hockey Hall of Fame*

brochures. Cartoons depicted long lineups at the Arena Gardens, with many fans not being able to get tickets for Leafs games. Smythe promised the new Gardens would have many more seats and fans wouldn't go home without a ticket. Cartoons showed wives of hockey fans who would rather go to games than stay at home. Smythe promised that the new Gardens would have so much room, the ladies of the city could also find tickets so they could join their husbands or enjoy a social evening with their friends.

History proves Smythe wasn't entirely accurate. Leafs tickets grew in popularity, and it actually became much more difficult to get tickets after the Gardens was completed than when the Leafs played at their old Mutual Street home. Still, these were examples of outstanding salesmanship. And Smythe was frank. In an open letter to fans, he pointed out that the new Madison Square Garden in New York and Boston Garden had given their home teams, the Americans, Rangers and Bruins, a financial advantage over the other teams, and if the Leafs were to compete, even survive, Toronto needed a hockey facility that would rival the new arenas in the United States. "In the Maple Leaf Club we were definitely faced with three alternatives," read the brochure. "First, give up major league hockey. Secondly, operate our team as cheaply as possible and 'get by' through selling the services of one or two players each year. Or thirdly, to sponsor and build a new arena ourselves."

In a comic strip in the brochure, the Stanley Cup was shown, filled with money, inside Boston Garden and Madison Square Garden. Both the Bruins and Rangers had recently won Cups, and Smythe tried to show fans that financial success made for success on the ice. "It certainly looks as if the Stanley Cup likes new and better homes—

and we sure do need an arena in Toronto," stated the strip's closing panel.

Even the site itself required a lot of salesmanship. In 1930, the land belonged to the Eaton's department store chain. The company had its main outlet less than a block from Church and Carlton. When Smythe and his financiers first approached Eaton's about buying the land, they were rebuffed. Eaton's felt hockey fans were low-class riffraff, that having hockey fans on its block would drive high-class, big-spending customers away. But, thanks to a hard-sell job from Smythe and his partners, Eaton's relented and sold the land in a $350,000 deal. Not only did Eaton's sell to Smythe, the company bought shares in the project and offered a sweetheart financing deal for the land, easing the financial pressure that would come when construction began.

But, despite raising over $1 million for the Gardens as of early 1931, Smythe and his partners were stunned when the cheapest tender for the project was a design from Ross and MacDonald Architects of Montreal, and with construction firm Thompson Brothers. That tender called for a budget of $1.5 million and, even though average working wages had fallen thanks to the Great Depression, Smythe and company didn't have the money.

Then came the final gamble. Selke was dispatched to meet with the construction workers with a unique proposal. As a union man, he knew that he would get an audience. He presented the workers the Maple Leafs' final offer. The project could still be saved if workers were willing to take a 20 per cent pay cut. In lieu of the pay cut, the workers would receive shares in the new building. The workers took the deal, and they were better off for it. The Gardens became such a profitable operation that they made back that 20 per cent many times over.

Because it was built on a shoestring budget, the Gardens never featured any opulent features. Truly, the project was a tribute to the working class. Completed in just over a summer, it opened its doors November 12, 1931, to a sold-out crowd of 13,542, well over the advertised capacity of 12,473. The top ticket went for $2.75. The building had no marble, no gold, no massive stone sculptures. Yellow brick, narrow windows and a tasteful domed roof highlighted what was really an economically built box. But the Leafs were a bad team. The team, coached by Art Duncan, lost the opener 2–1 to Chicago, and by the end of November were in last place in the league. So, Smythe fired Duncan and replaced him with Dick Irvin, who would turn the team around. Not only would Irvin turn the Leafs into a playoff team, he brought a championship to Toronto.

In 1932, at the end of the inaugural season at the Gardens, the Leafs beat the New York Rangers, the team that had fired Smythe the season before he acquired the St. Pats, so the boss got his sweet revenge. The Leafs swept the series in three games (back then, the Stanley Cup final was a best-of-five affair, not a best-of-seven as it is now) against a Rangers team that was similar to the squad Smythe first assembled in 1926. "I couldn't have written a better script myself," Smythe wrote in his memoirs.[3]

Oh, the memories the Gardens would produce. The Leafs would win 11 Stanley Cup finals while they called the building home. Bill Barilko scored the 1951 Stanley Cup winner in overtime at the Gardens, and it would be his last slap of the puck. He went missing after a bush plane he was in disappeared over northern Ontario that off-season.

His body would not be found for 11 years. In 1967, a Leafs team filled with veterans knocked off the defending champion Montreal Canadiens in six games. The Leafs, with an average age of 31, boasted the oldest roster to win a Cup in history. It would also mark the final time that the Leafs would win the Cup at the Gardens.

The Gardens also hosted maybe the most incredible night in NHL history when it comes to an individual record-setting night. On February 7, 1976, Maple Leafs

Punch Imlach embraces the Stanley Cup in 1962. *Archives of Ontario 10005427*

legend Darryl Sittler became the first NHLer and second major professional player to register 10 points in a game in an 11–4 win over the Boston Bruins. (Edmonton Oiler Jim Harrison did it in an 11–2 win over the New York Raiders in World Hockey Association action on January 30, 1973.)

Despite two major renovations, one in 1963 that added more than 2,000 seats to the Gardens, and another in 1986 that saw a new blue and white roof placed on the building, with a bold Maple Leafs logo that could be seen from aircraft passing overhead, the Gardens had become an albatross by the 1990s. This might not have been the case had city council not rejected a proposal made by the Leafs during the '60s that would have partially rebuilt the Gardens to a capacity of near 20,000. But, to make it work, the design required that the new Gardens have an overhang looming above city streets, and that wasn't popular with city politicians. Because the Gardens was part of an urban cityscape, there was nowhere else left to expand.

After Ballard's death in 1990, the Leafs once again became a team that concerned itself with more than putting fans' bums in the seats. It also wanted to win. But, the team needed the kind of revenue other clubs were getting from their sparkling new arenas—luxury boxes and capacities in the range of 20,000 fans. So, when the Leafs bought the basketball Raptors and the rights to their planned Air Canada Centre project, the writing was on the wall for hockey's grand old Gardens. It was the last of the Original Six rinks to survive, and it would close its doors to NHL hockey on February 13, 1999. The final game would see the Chicago Blackhawks, the same franchise that provided the opposition when the rink opened in 1931, take on the

A refreshment stand at the old Gardens, in an era before beer cost $13.50. *City of Toronto Archives, series 1057, item 7423*

Leafs in front of a sold-out house, and 104 members of the Leafs' alumni participated in a special closing ceremony after the final horn.

And, just as in '31, the visitors came out triumphant. The Hawks routed the Leafs 6–2, with goaltender Jocelyn Thibault getting the win. As a member of the Canadiens, Thibault was also the winning goalie in the last-ever game at the Montreal Forum, giving him a unique double in Canadian sports history.

The capacity at the final game was 15,726. Thanks to renovations made in the '60s, the building could seat more fans than it could when it opened.

The Gardens boasted outstanding sightlines thanks to the steep pitch of the seats—a climb up the greens or the greys was truly an athletic endeavour, up narrow stairways

The famous motto found in the Leafs' dressing room: "Defeat does not rest lightly on their shoulders." *City of Toronto Archives, series 1057, item 7448*

that asked for an aerobic effort. Because of the steep pitch, the end blue cheap seats were positioned very close to the glass, forcing fans to be extra aware of wayward shots that went out of play.

The Gardens even made the greatest player in the history of the game nostalgic. Wayne Gretzky spoke about the Gardens when his New York Rangers made their final visit there in the Christmas season of 1998–99. He first went to the Gardens as a child, when his grandmother took him to see his beloved Leafs take on the Oakland Seals. Gretzky would dazzle there in his career; his 77 points at the Gardens made him the highest-scoring visiting player in the history of the building. And Gretzky calls Game 7 of the 1993 Campbell Conference Final, which saw the Kings eliminate the Leafs, the finest game he ever played in the

NHL. Gretzky recalled how thrilled he was to play at the legendary shrine when he broke into the NHL with the Edmonton Oilers. "It's a tough situation in a lot of ways," said the Great One. "For the visitors, they have to come and play in front of the relatives. It's tough on the players... It was really intense for the guys who grew up in Ontario always wanting to play in Maple Leaf Gardens."

Foster Hewitt became a national icon calling games from the famed gondola at the Gardens. As the Gardens was being constructed, he looked down onto the site from an adjacent building and told Smythe he figured his best vantage point would come from a small "gondola" located 54 feet above the ice.

Maple Leaf Gardens was also the birthplace of the NHL All-Star Game in 1934. After Leafs star Ace Bailey's career was ended after a vicious hit from Boston Bruins legend Eddie Shore, a fundraiser was organized in honour of Bailey, where the Leafs, then the defending Cup holders, took on the All-Stars from the rest of the NHL. The Leafs prevailed by a 7–3 score. That was the genesis of the All-Star Game, now pretty much an annual NHL tradition (save for Olympic years). The Gardens would host seven more All-Star Games, with the final showcase coming in 1968.

The Gardens also hosted Game 2 of the famous '72 Summit Series, which saw the best Canadian NHL players take on the Russians. (It wasn't a true Canadian all-star team, as the NHL made it clear that players who defected to the World Hockey Association, including the great Bobby Hull, were not welcome on this sort-of Team Canada. If Canada had sent its best team available to it, then possibly the series may have not taken until late in the eighth game to decide.) After a 7–3 loss in Game 1 at the Montreal Forum, the Canadians stormed back for a 4–1 win at the Gardens, with Yvon Cournoyer scoring the winner.

It's hard not to notice that the Gardens didn't host many major NHL events after the '72 Summit Series. Ballard's ownership reign transformed the Leafs from the rivals of the Canadiens as the NHL's Cadillac franchise into doormats and, shamefully, laughingstocks. The Leafs made a couple of decent playoff runs, but truly got nowhere close to another Stanley Cup final after the '67 triumph. Ballard's famed hatred of Communism soon ruled the Gardens out as a place that welcomed the Russians or Czechoslovakians as international opponents for Canada.

But, Maple Leaf Gardens wasn't only the home of NHL-sanctioned events. The Toronto Huskies were a charter member of the National Basketball Association in 1946 and called the Gardens home. In fact, the Huskies' home opener against the New York Knicks was the first official regular-season game in NBA history.

The Toronto Marlboros, the famous junior team controlled by the Maple Leafs and winners of seven Memorial Cups before being moved to Hamilton during Ballard's reign as head of the franchise (the team later moved to Guelph in 1991, where the club is known as the Guelph Storm), began using the Gardens as its official home rink in 1963, even though the team used MLG for major games and finals since the building opened in 1931. In 1956, the Marlies faced the Regina Pats in the Memorial Cup final at the Gardens; the Marlies, defending champs, beat the Pats that season. In 1964, the Gardens had the unique privilege of hosting both the Memorial Cup and Stanley Cup winners in the same championship year. It marked the only time in history that both Canada's junior champion-ship and the NHL championship series were hosted by the same arena in the same season. In 1967, the Marlies and Leafs won their respective championships again, but this time the Marlies had to go on the road to do it.

John Bassett, after being frozen out of the Leafs' own-ership group, tried to bring another professional franchise to the Gardens. After a year at Varsity Arena, his Toronto Toros of the World Hockey Association moved to the Gardens for the 1974–75 season. The club featured ex-Leaf defensive stalwart Carl Brewer, but couldn't attract big crowds. After two seasons of playing to a half-full Gardens, the Toros moved to Birmingham, Alabama, in 1976 to become the Birmingham Bulls.

In early 2006, signs on the building boasted how Maple Leaf Gardens will soon be transformed into the ultimate grocery-shopping experience. The new Real Canadian Superstore to be built inside the old Gardens "will have lots of parking and a memorabilia museum highlighting the history of this great building," the sign read, slugged with the witty tag line, "Our bakery man-ager may get called for icing." But, in the autumn of 2006, those signs were taken down, replaced by simple blue signs that advertised the Gardens 75th anniversary.

While Loblaws' signage boasted that a new Superstore will be open in 2006, there has been no work done at the site as of the end of 2006, so at a glance it looks as if the goal of having a three-level store with underground parking in place by the original deadline will be missed. But, accord-ing to Geoff Wilson, the company's senior vice-president of investor relations and public affairs, "we are still in the pro-cess of finalizing design and construction details."

A faded Leafs logo on the media entrance near the corner of Church and Wood streets. *S. Sandor*

The Loblaws sale went through despite the protestations from Friends of Maple Leaf Gardens, a lobby group representing citizens who wanted to see the Gardens retain its primary function—to serve as a hockey shrine. Front and centre in the group was former Toronto mayor John Sewell. "What Friends of Maple Leaf Gardens presented was a plan that would compromise and place an ice surface in the grocery store," said Sewell. "We see great opportunity for junior, women's hockey. Community teams could play and have the thrill of playing at the Gardens which would have a configuration of 5,000."

Sewell and the Friends still lament the fact that their proposal to keep hockey at the Gardens got the support of only one member of council. And for that, he doesn't blame the City of Toronto as much as he does, ironically, the Maple Leafs. Sewell and the Friends believe that once the Leafs moved out for their new digs at the Air Canada

Centre, a building controlled by Maple Leaf Sports and Entertainment, they didn't want Maple Leaf Gardens as a competitor for concerts and other sports teams, such as lacrosse's Toronto Rock. "[MLSE President] Larry Tanenbaum controls the ACC and he doesn't want any competition," said Sewell. "He has the Leafs and Raptors and council says 'OK Larry, you get what you want.'"

One of the great things about the Gardens is that you could actually peer inside the arena through the glass main door that faced Carlton Street. Now, once through the doors, it's just a couple of steps up to the floor that was once the ice level. It is on this floor that film star Russell Crowe played a boxer in the 2005 film *Cinderella Man*. Gold and red seats still surround what was once the ice surface, but the cheaper green, grey and the end blue seats have been removed. The old art deco murals, painted in pastels and depicting greats of Leafs teams gone past, still adorn the lobby.

When it comes to our great sporting arenas, we are not very kind. We slap historical-site designations upon churches, famous homes, architecturally significant buildings. But, considering how large a role hockey has played in defining what it truly means to be Canadian, it's galling to think that so many of our great rinks have gone. The old Arena Gardens, where the Leafs first played, is gone. The shell of the old Montreal Forum remains, but the inside was gutted to make way for a shopping galleria known as the Pepsi Forum Entertainment Centre.

It's no different in the USA; old famous ballparks like Ebbets Field in Brooklyn and New York's Polo Grounds were reduced to rubble. Boston Garden, more famous with Americans because of the exploits of the Celtics basketball dynasty rather than hockey's big, bad, Bruins, is nothing but a memory. Considering how sporting shrines are usually destroyed once the tenants move out, maybe the Loblaws grocery chain's plan for a Superstore with a museum on site is the best fate hockey historians can hope for.

How to Get There

To get to the Gardens, take the subway to College. Walk a block east down Carlton, or take the 506 streetcar one stop east to Church Street. After having a look at the Gardens, why not check out the Leafs' original Arena Gardens home on Mutual Street? It's just a quick walk south down to the corner of Church and Dundas; the old Mutual Street Arena was on the next intersection to the east.

It May be Small, But It's a Major Venue: St. Michael's College Arena

There is no escaping the irony—Canada's largest city is home to the smallest arena in major junior hockey.

To say that the old rink located on the grounds of St. Michael's College School is cozy would be an understatement. At just 180 feet by 80 feet, the ice is much smaller than the North American hockey accepted dimensions of 200 feet by 85 feet. There are just six rows of bench seats on each side of the rink, with rails for standing room behind. There's a scattering of seats behind the end boards, maybe two rows' worth. All told, when St. Michael's Arena is full, with the three suites and media box jammed, it can hold 1,600 fans. It is easily the most intimate atmosphere in Canadian junior hockey. Compare St. Mike's to junior teams in Vancouver and Calgary, which play in NHL-size arenas and regularly draw crowds of more than 10,000, with tickets to spare.

But, while St. Michael's Arena is the smallest rink in Canadian major junior hockey, it might also be the most storied rink in Canadian junior hockey. St. Michael's, the famous Catholic high school boys academy, has been associated with putting elite teams on the ice for a century.

The photographs that line the arena walls are proof of the tradition of excellence at St. Mike's. As soon as a St. Mike's grad, either from the Majors, the Junior "A" Buzzers or the high school Double Blue teams, makes it to the NHL, his picture goes up on the arena wall. As of the 2006 off-season, 174 photos of men who once wore the double-blue St. Mike's jersey, with that oh-so-famous-yet-simple bold "M" logo on the chest, have gone on to the NHL, from Reg Noble, the Hall of Famer who made his debut in the very first days of the National Hockey League, to modern superstars such as former NHL MVP Eric Lindros, Ottawa Senators' sniper Jason Spezza and goalie Sean Burke. The wall even includes a picture of Don Keenan, who played just one NHL game—March 7, 1959, for the Boston Bruins. Keenan, who was with St. Mike's program at the time, was called up to be an emergency injury fill-in for a game at Maple Leaf Gardens, and was saddled with a 4–1 loss.

Once you walk through the front doors of the building, take a swift turn into the lounge. At the far end you'll find 12 plaques dedicated to the dozen St. Mike's alumni who have earned hockey's highest honour—enshrinement in the Hockey Hall of Fame. You'll see Noble; early hockey legend Frank Rankin; "Gentleman" Joe Primeau, the anchor of the famous Maple Leafs "Kid Line" of the 1930s; Red Wings legend "Terrible" Ted Lindsay; Leafs and Red Wings standout Leonard "Red" Kelly; Tim Horton, maybe the best defenceman to ever wear the Maple Leafs jersey and Canadian doughnut-chain patriarch; Frank Mahovlich, whose No. 27 can be found in the rafters of the Air Canada Centre; Gerry Cheevers, the Boston Bruins famed goalie of the '70s; Dave Keon, perhaps the most talented player to ever wear the Leafs' sweater; Bobby Bauer, a member of the Bruins' legendary "Kraut Line" of the '30s; Father David Bauer, St. Mike's famous mentor; and Murray Costello, the grad who was inducted in 2005 as a builder.

This arena was completed in 1960. At that time, the Majors, founded in 1906 by Fr. Henry Carr, had already established itself as Canada's most elite junior program that mixed academics with hockey. Players attended the school and played hockey in their off-academic hours. While some players went on to stardom with the other five of the Original Six teams, St. Mike's was truly a feeder program of the Maple Leafs; the program was one of two—the junior Toronto Marlboros was the other—heavily bank-rolled by Leafs' owner Conn Smythe.

The fact that Conn Smythe's Maple Leafs financed the Majors' program throughout its glory days flies in the face of one of the most famous assumptions about the old Leafs patriarch—that he was a staunch anti-Catholic. If this was true, why did the Leafs have such strong ties with a Catholic academy? But Les Duff, who played with St. Mike's in the early '50s and is the brother of former Leafs star Dick Duff, said that even though Maple Leaf Gardens financially supported the St. Mike's program, Majors play-ers had a lot harder time catching the eyes of the Leafs brass than did the non-Catholic Marlies players. "Every year it seemed that seven Marlies would go to the Leafs, and they'd take only one St. Mike's player," said Duff.

Anti-Catholic feelings were not uncommon in the Protestant Ontario of the 1950s. Even though St. Mike's boasted one of the proudest junior hockey programs in the country, players would often be ridiculed for playing for a Catholic school. "I remember playing in Barrie and their fans threw little fish, like anchovies, down on the ice at us," said Duff. "It was terrible."

Before 1960, neither St. Mike's nor the Toronto Marlboros had a permanent home; they would often have

Dick and Les Duff, brothers playing for St. Mike's in the glory days. *Courtesy Les Duff*

their major junior match-ups scheduled as doubleheaders at Maple Leaf Gardens. Why did the Leafs fund two teams? Because it would give the club an even deeper pool of top young talent from which to cherry-pick players— and it would allow the Catholic players who caught their eye to attend a Catholic academy. The split was simple: if a prospect was Catholic, he was sent to the Majors; if he wasn't a Catholic, he went to the Marlies.

When St. Mike's finally finished construction on its own home in 1960, the team was already the stuff of legend, having won three Memorial Cups (in 1934, '45 and '47) and an Allan Cup in 1910 as Canada's men's amateur champs.

That first Memorial Cup, Canada's junior championship, remains legendary. St. Mike's was led by Bobby Bauer, who would go on to become a Boston Bruins legend. After blistering through the Eastern Canada playdowns, St. Mike's met the Edmonton Athletics, a team that would go on to make up most of the roster of the Edmonton Flyers club that would win the Allan Cup of 1948. After blowing out the Athletics 5–0 in Game 1 of the best-of-three series, Game 2 went into double overtime. Games were not sudden-death affairs back then, so St. Mike's got two goals in the second overtime frame to win 6–4 and clinch the championship.

The arena officially opened with an exhibition game between the current Majors and the St. Mike's alumni on November 7, 1960. The "Old Boys" alumni team featured legends Keon, Mahovlich and Horton, with Primeau doing the coaching. The Majors junior team, coached by Fr. Bauer, featured Cheevers in goal.

Fr. Bauer began coaching St. Mike's in 1953, returning to the school in which he starred as a player before going off to be ordained. Duff remembers Bauer as a coach with some rather unorthodox ideas—ideas that were years ahead of their time. "He'd tell us to look two or three feet ahead," Duff recalled. "He'd tell us all to kick stones ahead of us, and look at how they skipped ahead of our feet. He had us all doing that, and we must have all looked crazy." But it was done to train the young Majors in the art of anticipating where the puck would go on the ice, not to react to where it is on the ice.

Duff recalled that, even before Bauer returned to St. Mike's to coach the Majors, the priests had a great deal of influence on the team. The players were required to go to morning masses. Marks were strictly monitored, and practices were held right after school finished. "If we swore just once on the ice, it was right to the prinicipal's office," he said.

But some of the boys did try to stretch the rules. Duff can still remember the time that then-St. Mike's teammate Reggie Fleming, who went on to play for six NHL teams through the '60s and '70s, snuck into the priest's side of the confession booth, and actually took confessions from other players.

Bauer wasn't the only revolutionary hockey thinker involved with St. Mike's. The players were also trained by legendary Canadian fitness guru Lloyd Percival. When he wrote *The Hockey Handbook* in 1951, Percival's ideas of how the game should be played and how players should train were laughed off by North American coaches. But Soviet coaches found his ideas fascinating, and soon, the concept of five-man units (still used by the Russians today) caused a hockey renaissance behind the Iron Curtain. Many of Percival's legendary hockey ideas were hatched at St. Mike's practices on the old outdoor rink that was replaced by the modern arena—or at practices at the old Leaside Arena or the University of Toronto's Varsity Arena, which the school also used.

Duff recalls getting a terrible charley horse after both of his thighs were clipped by an opposing player's knees. He was in agony, but Percival got him ready for the next game by standing in front of a fireplace and then doing sprints up and down a flight of stairs, in order to promote blood flow and break up the bruising and swelling.

Percival was a fitness nut in an era when hockey players though the term "off-ice workout" meant going out for a night on the town. At practices at Maple Leaf Gardens, he would make each and every player skate a dozen hard laps, save for star forward Bill Dineen, who would be forced to skate two dozen laps. That was back in '53, and it must have worked; Dineen graduated to the NHL's Detroit Red Wings the next year and ended up winning two Stanley Cups there.

By the spring of 1961, that St. Mike's team would add the fourth Memorial Cup to the school's very cluttered trophy case. The Memorial Cup final would go to six games, but the Majors triumphed over the Edmonton Oil Kings with a 4–2 win in what would turn out to be the series decider.

Ironically, in the 1961 off-season, the school decided to withdraw from top-level junior hockey, as it felt that the demands of a busy junior schedule were taking away from the boys' academic performance. Fr. Bauer, who also won the Memorial Cup as an Oshawa Generals' player in 1944, would leave the school and eventually help found the Canadian national team program. His contributions to hockey are just as famous in the West as they are in Toronto; a rink in Calgary, the current home of Hockey Canada, bears his name. Bauer's name is also legendary at the University of British Columbia, where he coached. Not only is he a Hall of Famer, Fr. Bauer was also made a member of the Order of Canada.

Even though St. Mike's abandoned major junior hockey, the St. Mike's Arena still played host to the school's Junior "A" club, the Buzzers, as well as St. Mike's high school teams, the senior and junior Double Blue squads. Those teams still exist today.

For 36 years, major junior hockey and St. Mike's were

separate. In 1997, though, through the help of private investors, the Majors were relaunched. Why? Because at the time there was no major junior hockey being played within Toronto city limits. In 1989, late Maple Leafs owner Harold Ballard decided to move the Marlboros down the Queen Elizabeth Way to Hamilton, where the team would be known as the Dukes, thus killing junior hockey in the city. With no Ontario Hockey League team in Toronto, investors felt the time was right to bring back the Majors name. In 1997, the Majors made their debut, with plans to make a temporary home at the St. Mike's Arena. Nine years later the team, which was purchased in 2000 by school alumnus Eugene Melnyk, has finally found its new home out in the suburbs, and it hopes to move there in 2007–08. "It is no secret that we want to move into a larger arena," said Parker Neale, the Majors' media and public relations director.

In the 2006 off-season, Melnyk purchased the troubled Mississauga IceDogs franchise, which makes its home

The Majors face the Ottawa 67's in OHL action. *Courtesy Toronto-St. Michael's Majors*

just outside of Toronto's western borders at the ultra-modern Hershey Centre. Melnyk was given permission by the Ontario Hockey League to make the move under the condition he sell the IceDogs as quickly as possible to an investor who wants to move the franchise to a new community. Once the IceDogs sale and move is complete, St. Mike's will move to Mississauga. For sure, St. Mike's will play at the old arena for the 2006–07 season, but it's likely that it will be the final campaign the franchise will play inside the city's borders.

Neale said that Melnyk, who also paid for the complete renovation of the school's football facility—which sits right next to the arena—is a proud St. Mike's grad, and wants to keep the team name and logos after the move. Of course, Melnyk, who made his fortune in the pharmaceutical business, is more famous with Canadian hockey fans as being the owner of the Ottawa Senators.

Melnyk did consider a purchase of Maple Leaf Gardens, to keep the grand old building alive as a hockey facility. But Maple Leaf Sports and Entertainment, which would later sell the building to Loblaws, informed Melnyk that it was not interested in selling the old barn to him. Of course, as the Senators have surpassed the Montreal Canadiens as the Leafs most bitter rivals, it would have been an uncomfortable deal, with the owner of the Sens controlling the spiritual home of the Maple Leafs. But, the hockey purist will argue that reuniting the Majors with the Gardens, the arena in which the team had many of its glorious moments, would have been a win-win situation for the city. As well, MLSE did not want the Gardens, a building it once owned, competing with its new Air Canada Centre for concerts and other non-hockey sporting events, such as basketball and lacrosse.

In a statement made to clarify his offer, Melnyk pledged the Gardens would only be used for minor and amateur hockey. "I have said—and will now say again—that I am prepared to sign a deal that would commit to not hosting concerts or other entertainment beyond the thrills of minor hockey," said Melnyk in a written statement released in 2004. "I am also prepared to consider any other criteria that may be put on the table—as long as I can save the Gardens and give our kids the privilege of playing on the same ice as minor hockey and NHL greats such as Tim Horton, Frank Mahovlich, Red Kelly and Dave Keon.

"Preserving the facade of Maple Leaf Gardens is not enough. The historical importance of the Gardens has less to do with its exterior. It's all about the inside—the aura and spirit of a building that played host to events which are deeply significant to preserving Toronto's history—from Ali to Elvis to 11 Stanley Cup Championships. If you don't believe me, just look at the Montreal Forum. Its history is now largely lost and displaced by movie theatres. I strongly believe that we need to preserve our hockey history in Toronto."

Those don't sound like the words of a hostile Senators owner. To be fair to Melnyk, it needs to be noted that his interest in the Gardens pre-dated his decision to purchase the Sens.

Time is running out to see major junior hockey being played in this very tiny, very intimate venue. Unlike the first incarnation of the Majors, the team is privately owned, carrying the name as more of a tribute to the famous academy than a practical association. In fact, in the 2005–06 season, only one Major actually went to St. Mike's, but, while in most other junior franchises players have to put off post-secondary education until after their careers are done—if they don't go on to the pro ranks, that is—many Majors players attend Toronto's colleges or universities while they play.

The new Majors have yet to win the Memorial Cup, but, before being eliminated in the first round of the OHL playoffs in 2006, the team had gone to four conference finals in a row.

Like the Majors, the modern Buzzers are privately owned, and are required to have 51 per cent of their roster be either St. Mike's students or grads. But the Buzzers continue on in the same proud tradition as when the team was founded by the school in 1933. The Buzzers won the Frank L. Buckland Trophy as champions of the Ontario Provincial Junior "A" Hockey League in 2005 and 2006. Before joining the Junior "A" ranks, the Buzzers won the Sutherland Cup as Ontario Junior "B" champs in '34, '36, '45, '61, '82 and '89.

With the two high school Double Blue teams also in place, there is no danger of St. Mike's divorcing itself from hockey anytime soon. Whether you go to see major junior, Junior "A" or high school hockey at this tiny arena, the motto emblazoned over the front entrance, "Teach me goodness, discipline and knowledge," will undoubtedly grab your attention.

St. Mike's alumni remain close to their old school and junior program. During the 2004-05 lockout, former St. Mike's and Toronto Maple Leafs greats Dick Duff and Leonard "Red" Kelly brought the Stanley Cup to St. Mike's Arena for a visit.

Need Tickets?

You would think that, at an arena as small as St. Mike's, tickets would be at a premium. Sadly, this isn't the case. As with the Marlies of the American Hockey League, the

Majors struggle to capture the attention of Torontonians, who focus all of their hockey passion on the Maple Leafs. The rink is rarely full, so chances are you can walk up and get tickets.

The box office opens two hours before game time, and tickets can be had for less than $20 each. For the 2006–07 season, the Majors advertised a full season ticket on the rail (best seats in the house) for $510, good for 34 home games in an Ontario Hockey League season. That's about the same price you'd pay for two good seats at the Air Canada Centre for a single Leafs game. If the Majors vacate the rink, Buzzers and Double Blue games will still keep the arena going.

How to Get There

The St. Michael's College School Arena is easy to find. Take the subway to St. Clair West subway station (basically located underneath a Loblaws supermarket superstore). The arena is directly behind the supermarket, at 1515 Bathurst Street.

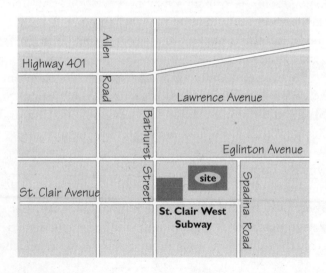

Lakeshore Lions Arena:
The Leafs' Home Away From Home

Tucked inside the southwest city limits, sitting on the north shore of Lake Ontario, lies Mimico, a gritty industrial neighbourhood known for its blue-collar residents, train yards, factories and brownstones that dot Lake Shore Boulevard. It is common to hear Polish being spoken on Mimico streets and there are a variety of excellent European delicatessens and bakeries that have cropped up in the Lakeshore Village shopping area.

The fact that Mimico offers the best views of the lake in the entire city is a well-kept secret. Except for a few posh developments towards the Humber River to the east, the lakefront high-rise has not replaced most of the walk-ups built in the post-Second World War era.

Mimico's working-class ethic is best reflected in the neighbourhood's most famous hockey export, Brendan Shanahan, who will one day see his name on a plaque in the Hockey Hall of Fame.

In 1997, after winning his first of three Stanley Cups with the Detroit Red Wings, Shanahan brought the famous mug to the Blue Goose, a small tavern located across the street from the Mimico railway station. The Goose is the gathering place for hockey players and fans throughout the area. The tavern also held a welcome home party in 2006 for David Bolland, the local product who was a key part of the Canadian national team that won the World Junior title in Vancouver that year. Bolland actually snuck into Shanahan's Cup party at the Goose a decade before, so he could get a glimpse of hockey's holy grail.

Go a few blocks west of Mimico station and, on non-game days during homestands, you will have a good chance at spotting a few Maple Leafs in the area.

The Air Canada Centre is a multipurpose facility. Not only is it home to the Maple Leafs, but also to the basketball Raptors, the Rock of the National Lacrosse League and a full slate of concerts and special events. So, chances are, if the Leafs don't have a home game, somebody else has got the ACC booked. The Leafs spend most of their off-days in Toronto practicing at the Lakeshore Lions Arena, found where New Toronto meets Mimico, near the corner of Lake Shore Boulevard and Kipling Avenue.

Located deep in the city's west end, away from the subway line, the facility allows the Leafs the chance to get away from the centre of the city and the prying eyes of fans.

The Lakeshore Lions Arena in 2007. It will soon be replaced by a multi-rink mega-complex.
S. Sandor

If you are not a member of the accredited media, the only way to get into practice is with the special permission of the hockey team. That's not to say the Leafs' inhabitation of this community rink is done with the doors always closed. During the off-season, the team has a tradition of hosting a summer hockey camp at the Arena, where Atom, Novice and Pee Wee-aged players can learn from Leafs past and present as well as the coaching staff.

The Leafs have always had a special bond with the west end of the city. Conn Smythe lived in the west near the corner of Bloor and Jane Streets. When Smythe took over the franchise in the late '20s, the Ravina Gardens, located near High Park, was the team's chosen practice site. Lakeshore Lions Arena only continues the tradition of the Leafs holding workouts in the west end or Etobicoke.

The arena was not built with the Leafs in mind; it was the product of nearly four years worth of fundraising and planning by the local chapter of the Lions' Club. It was felt that teams in New Toronto and Mimico, bustling western suburbs of Toronto after the end of the Second World War, needed an indoor facility with artificial ice that could rival the arenas found in the centre of Toronto.

The Lakeshore Lions Arena opened on February 1, 1951, with between 1,150 and 1,200 fans jamming the place to see the first-ever hockey game to be contested on the new building's artificial sheet. They went home happy as the New Toronto Ostranders, the local Ontario Hockey Association intermediate team, beat the Oakville Lakeshores by a 4–1 count. A local kid named Stan Milne was the first star of the Lakeshore Lions Arena, scoring twice to pace the Ostranders to the win.

Lakeshore Lions Arena has also been the home rink

of the Ryerson University Rams team; but, in 2005, the school, which is located in the heart of downtown, decided to move the team to the George Bell Arena, located closer to the core and within a subway ride of the student body.

The Lakeshore Lions Arena will soon be replaced. With continued growth in the west end and the Leafs continuing their commitment to keep their practice facility in the southwest corner of the city, a new $29 million Lakeshore Lions complex with four ice surfaces, one of them Olympic-sized, is expected to be ready for 2008. In September of 2006, city council approved the new arena by a 36–3 vote. The Lions Club pays for the arena, but the Leafs and its farm team, the Marlies, will agree to pay annual rent of $500,000 per season.

The Leafs are currently in full support of the new arena plan, but it wasn't their first choice. As much as the team has been linked to practice arenas in the west end through its history, it had hoped to secure a practice facility closer to downtown. In 2003, the Leafs were hopeful to piggyback onto the construction of a new arena at the University of Toronto as part of a planned new stadium project. "We've got a short-term [solution] at Lakeshore Lions, which is great," Maple Leaf Sports and Entertainment President Richard Peddie said in 2003.[1] "But we're looking for something more central and we're also looking for something we can also use, not only as a practice facility, but something we can use for our community events and sponsor events. Something that is more ambitious than just a hockey facility."

When the U of T plan fell through, staying in Etobicoke became the best option for the club, and the building of the new arena is going to allow the remainder of Peddie's vision, save for the central location, to be realized.

How to Get There

Take the subway to Kipling station. From there, get on the 44 Kipling South bus. (Do not get on the 45 Kipling, it goes north, not south!) Take the bus to Birmingham Street. The arena is about a block west of the intersection of Kipling and Birmingham, adjacent to Lakeshore Collegiate School. If you want to see the Goose, get off at Royal York station and take the 76 Royal York South bus to Mimico GO station; you can see the tavern from there.

Or, from downtown, you can take the 501 Long Branch streetcar west to either Royal York Road or Kipling Avenue, and take the corresponding 44 or 76 buses that will get you where you want to go. The streetcar offers a scenic ride through Toronto's west end, but be warned: streetcar service in Toronto, especially for a trip this long, is somewhat unreliable. Streetcars are vulnerable to long delays in traffic tie-ups and are often overcrowded. As well, do not even look at the streetcar schedules posted at the stops. Experienced commuters know that these collections of names and numbers are urban hieroglyphs, difficult to read and with no relevance whatsoever to the modern world.

Lionel Conacher Park:
Celebrating Toronto's First Family of Hockey

Today, Toronto's Summerhill neighbourhood is a pretty pricey place to live, filled with upscale townhouses and condos, and chic shopping. Located just north of Rosedale and just a couple of subway stops from Yorkville—and just a little south of Forest Hill—Summerhill has taken its place as one of Toronto's preferred neighbourhoods.

Walking through Summerhill, it might be difficult to imagine that this was once a tough, working-class neighbourhood. But, at the beginning of the 20th century, those

Lionel Conacher's monument at the centre of Lionel Conacher Park. *N. Der*

tony townhouses were simple abodes for families looking to scrape by.

And it was in this working-class Summerhill area where Toronto's most famous hockey family learned to skate and develop their love for the game. Brothers Lionel, Charlie and Roy Conacher grew up in Summerhill and all went on to legendary hockey careers. Lionel "The Big Train" Conacher was the most famous of the three—and it is for him that Lionel Conacher Park, located just a few blocks from where he and his famous brothers grew up, stands today.

Lionel was not only a National Hockey League star, but also a multi-sport wonder. In 1950, he was named Canada's Athlete of the Half Century. The "Big Train" was a rugged football running back, and his crowning moment came in the 1921 Grey Cup, where he was the driving force behind the Toronto Argonauts' triumph over the Edmonton Eskimos. Legend has it, the same day he played in the Grey Cup, Conacher also skated for the amateur Aura Lee hockey club in a game against the Toronto Granites.

Conacher was also a national boxing champion, a lacrosse star who was part of the provincial-title-winning Maitlands team, and a good baseball player. Conacher was part of the Maple Leafs baseball team that won a Triple A title in 1926. Historians, unfortunately, have exaggerated Conacher's role with the team. He only played three games with the Leafs and never got a hit, so his role in the championship was very minor.

The park itself is simple—a playground for kids and a little block of green space perfect for walking the dog. But, in the northeast corner of the park you will find a stone monument dedicated to The Big Train. Unfortunately,

The Conacher brothers (left to right): Charlie, Roy and Lionel. *Hockey Hall of Fame*

there are white squiggles of spray paint on the stone, added by a really bad graffiti artist. The monument dedicated by the Province of Ontario in October of 1967 not only commemorates Conacher as a hockey, football, baseball, boxing and lacrosse star, but also notes that he served as both an Ontario MPP and a federal MP after his sports-playing days were over.

Check that. The Big Train's sports-playing days never ended. He actually died in 1954 of a heart attack suffered while running the basepaths in a charity softball game.

One year before winning the Grey Cup with the football Argos, The Big Train made his mark as a hard-hitting defenceman with the Toronto Canoe Club Paddlers junior hockey club. In 1920, the Paddlers became the second team ever to capture the Memorial Cup, the new trophy awarded to Canada's junior champions.

NHL teams were interested, but Conacher's passion for football, lacrosse and baseball would not allow him to commit to one sport. So, he remained an amateur. Eventually, he went to the United States to play with the Pittsburgh Pirates, an amateur club that won a pair of American amateur titles before becoming an NHL expansion club in 1925. It was with the Pirates' move from amateur to pro ranks that Conacher finally became an NHLer.

Within a year, Conacher joined the New York Americans. He was not only the No. 1 defenceman on the team, but the coach as well. It was on Broadway that he would develop into an All-Star defender. Conacher was never what anyone would consider an offensive force—11 goals was his best-ever total—but his smarts and physical play got him a reputation as a tough SOB who could rival the Bruins' Eddie Shore when it came to grit.

After leaving the Americans in 1930, he would play seven more NHL seasons, six of them with the Montreal Maroons. But, in his one year outside of Montreal, he led the Chicago Black Hawks to a Stanley Cup in 1934. He then returned to Montreal and won a Cup with the Maroons in 1935.

It would be unfair to visit Lionel Conacher's monument on Birch Avenue without thinking of his famous hockey-playing brothers. After all, all three are members of the Hockey Hall of Fame. And, it can be argued that, when it came to a talent for hockey, Lionel trailed Charlie and Roy. Lionel only began playing hockey seriously while in his late teens, and only chose an NHL career over football or lacrosse because, at that time, pro hockey players received bigger paycheques than athletes in most other pro leagues. Meanwhile, Charlie and Roy began skating when they were kids—they knew from day one that hockey was their game.

While Lionel was named athlete of the half century and has a park named in his honour, most Torontonians associate the Conacher name with Charlie, the brother known as "The Big Bomber" for his vicious shot, who starred with the hometown Leafs. A banner in honour of Charlie still hangs today from the rafters of the Air Canada Centre. Conacher and Harvey "Busher" Jackson were the stars of the Toronto Marlies team that won the Memorial Cup in 1929. The two were brought up to the Leafs together and were joined with Joe Primeau to make up the "Kid Line," one of the most famous troikas in not only Leafs history, but NHL history.

Five times between the 1929–30 and 1935–36 seasons, Charlie was the top goal-scorer in the NHL. He was named an All-Star five times and won two Art Ross Trophies as the league's top point-getter. Oh, he and the Leafs took the Cup in 1932. He finished his career with the Detroit Red Wings and New York/Brooklyn Americans, but his goal-scoring exploits will forever make him a Maple Leafs legend.

Roy was a sensation before he reached the NHL. He starred as a teenager with the vaunted St. Mike's program before graduating to the West Toronto Nationals, which he led to a title as Memorial Cup Champions in 1936. As a rookie with the Boston Bruins in the 1938–39 season, Roy entered the NHL with a bang. With 26 goals in 47 games,

Charlie Conacher, local hockey hero, graces the cover of a game program from the '30s. *Hockey Hall of Fame*

he was the league's top lamp-lighter. He led the Bruins to the Cup final where they would face the Maple Leafs, who had sent Charlie to the Red Wings a season before. Roy would get a measure of revenge for the Conacher clan, scoring the Cup winner.

Roy would win two Cups with the Bruins before going into the military, and after the Second World War, he established himself as one of the league's top scorers with both the Detroit Red Wings and the Chicago Black Hawks. In 1948–49, Roy captured the Art Ross Trophy as the NHL's top point-getter, with 68 in 60 games for the Hawks. When he called it quits, he averaged nearly a point per game through his 11-season NHL career. With scoring totals of that era, that was a significant feat.

So, Lionel Conacher Park should not only be a tribute to one member of the family, but to all three brothers. All in the Hall of Fame. Five Stanley Cups. Each brother won a Memorial Cup. And, seven decades after they ruled the NHL, they are still Toronto's first family of hockey.

How to Get There

Getting to Lionel Conacher Park is easy. Take the subway to Summerhill station. When you get to the surface, you will find yourself on Shaftesbury Avenue just east of Yonge Street. Cross to the west side of Yonge Street and walk south. The next intersection (before the bridge) is Birch Avenue. Turn right and walk a block and the park—and monument—are right there.

As well, Lionel and Charlie opened a service station at the corner of Yonge and Davenport while they were NHL stars, banking that drivers would want to come to their spot so they could brag that they were gassed up by the sporting legends. That intersection is just three blocks north of Yonge/Bloor station on the subway, right at the edge of the oh-so-ritzy Yorkville district.

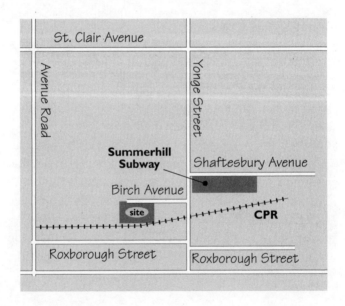

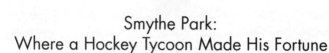

Smythe Park:
Where a Hockey Tycoon Made His Fortune

Smythe Park isn't a notable hockey site because a major game was played there.

This beautiful wildlife reserve, filled with ponds and creeks perfect for the hundreds of ducks and geese that call it home, is worthy of note for the hockey fan because it sits on the site of the old sand and gravel pit on which Conn Smythe transformed himself from a war hero into a tycoon, with enough wealth to at least make a starting bid for a National Hockey League franchise. And that he did

The Scarlett Road entrance to Smythe Park. *N. Der*

in 1927 when he bought the Toronto St. Pats, and transformed them into the Toronto Maple Leafs.

C. Smythe for Sand was formed in 1920 after Smythe, fresh out of the First World War, bought an old truck. He would then partner with Frank Angotti, who had just entered the paving business. They would later divorce, with Smythe taking the sand business and Angotti keeping the paving side. But, it was while they were together that they bought this plot of land northwest of Toronto (the site now falls well within the city boundaries).

So desperate were the pair to start the business, they started shoveling material out of the ground as soon as the deeds were signed, without going to the city for necessary permits, gambling that no one would complain.

As the gravel pit began to turn a profit, Smythe remained involved in hockey by coaching at his alma mater, the University of Toronto. Before going off to war, Smythe was a solid part of the varsity team. He showed that he was an even better hockey brain than he was a player; under his leadership, the U of T won six Ontario Hockey Association titles in the 1920s. His Grads team would go on to win the Allan Cup in 1927, symbolic of Canadian amateur hockey supremacy. That same team would go on to win gold at the 1928 Winter Olympics, but Smythe, who was then involved with the day-to-day operations of a National Hockey League franchise, was not there to savour the win.

As the U of T hockey program flourished under Smythe, C. Smythe for Sand prospered. This small strip of land would help Smythe provide seed money not only to buy the St. Pats, but to build Maple Leaf Gardens in 1931. This pit was also put forward as a reason that Smythe chose to hold the New York Rangers' inaugural training

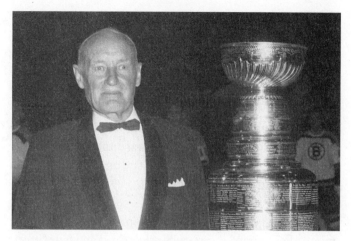

Conn Smythe with the Stanley Cup. *Hockey Hall of Fame*

camp in Toronto's Ravina Gardens back in 1926. It was reported that Smythe didn't want to spend too much time away from his business, which paid him quite a bit more than the expansion NHL team was giving him.

Eventually, Smythe would move his family close to his business. The Smythes would finally settle at 68 Baby Point Road as the city expanded northward. The house is located just a few blocks from the Park/old pit.

The park, opened in 1977 (three years before Smythe's death) is about as good an example of returning an industrial site to nature as you will find in the Greater Toronto Area. In fact, Smythe Park was awarded a Bronze Plaque Award, given for excellence in land reclamation by the Aggregate Producer's Association of Ontario. So good is the restoration that it's impossible to tell that this was once a gravel pit, save for the fact the park is situated in a ravine, set below Scarlett Road to the west and Jane Street to the east.

Smythe Park is just one example of how Smythe's legacy continues to thrive in Toronto thanks to the philanthropy he displayed during his lifetime. The Conn Smythe Dinner, which features top sports celebrities, is one of the top annual charitable functions in the city, and the money goes to the Easter Seals Kids fund. Smythe was also a staunch supporter of the Ontario Association for the Deaf. That's worth remembering when you are watching honking geese and quacking ducks floating in the stream and park named for Toronto's godfather of hockey.

How to Get There

Smythe Park sprawls between Scarlett Road and Jane Street, so you can use either street's bus route to get there. The 79 Scarlett bus leaves from Runnymede subway station. Once the bus joins Scarlett Road, look for the Lambton Golf and Country Club to your left. The park is on your right. Or, you could use the 35 Jane bus, which loads at Jane subway station. Once you cross Woolner Avenue, look for the park on your left.

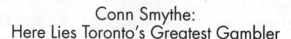

Conn Smythe:
Here Lies Toronto's Greatest Gambler

As you walk into Park Lawn Cemetery, at the corner of Bloor Street and Prince Edward Drive in Toronto's well-to-do Kingsway district, it's hard not to notice the amount of money people will spend on death. Obelisks in the middle of the cemetery can easily be seen from the gates, as can large stone crosses that sit on top of gravestones that are taller than the average human being.

Of course, you would assume that the grave of Conn Smythe, the man who built the Toronto Maple Leafs, the

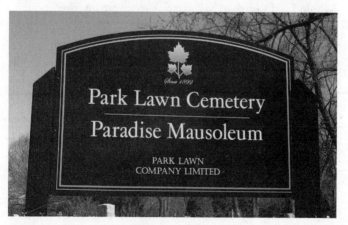

The gates of Park Lawn Cemetery, from Prince Edward Drive. *S. Sandor*

man who built Maple Leaf Gardens, would be marked by one of the showiest stones of all.

But that's not the case. Smythe's grave, located in Section G, plot 315, is surprising in its simplicity. A nondescript grey stone marks Smythe (born February 1, 1895, died November 18, 1980), his wife Irene Eleanor Sands, and their daughter Constance Patricia ("Patricia" to her mom and dad), who died in 1945 at the family cottage in Orchard Beach at just 10 years of age. Despite her tender age, she suffered a fatal heart attack, brought on by an allergic reaction.

But it's truly fitting that the grave of the man who transformed a struggling National Hockey League team known as the Toronto St. Pats into the empire that is the Toronto Maple Leafs is simple. That's because the true monument to his life is the hockey palace on the corner of Church and Carlton. Like architect Christopher Wren, who never wanted a showy headstone because he wanted to be remembered in death for London's St. Paul's Cathedral, Maple Leaf Gardens is Smythe's more fitting memorial.

Unlike most men who enter the world of major professional sports ownership, Smythe did not already have a massive fortune in hand when he took on the Toronto St. Pats. But Smythe was a gambler through and through—fitting for a man who would also later serve as a director on the Ontario Jockey Club board and would see horses from his stable win the Queen's Plate, Canada's top thoroughbred racing prize.

When he purchased the Toronto St. Pats in 1927 for the sum of $200,000, he needed the help of partners. He had made his name as a successful manager and coach of the University of Toronto, but his reign as the manager of

Section G, plot 315—the Smythe family grave. *S. Sandor*

the New York Rangers, cut short after one training camp in 1926, had left him bitter. He had a successful contracting, sand and gravel business and was easily someone a person would call wealthy, but definitely not stinking rich. In fact, he took the severance money from the Rangers and successfully bet it against the result of a U of T football game just to earn the initial payment on the Toronto club. He would then take that money and bet it again on an NHL game, winning both bets to get the funds needed to at least get a deal moving.

When the Ottawa Senators demanded the then-unheard-of sum of $35,000 for defenceman Francis "King" Clancy back in 1930, and the Leafs board of directors could not come up with the money to match the offer, Smythe went to the old Woodbine racetrack to bet on his horse, Rare Jewel. He won over $15,000 in wagers and prizes, enough to make the deal happen.

The Gardens itself was a major gamble. He sold shares with the enthusiasm of a street hawker in order to raise the money needed to build the arena. In fact, Smythe, his shareholders and partners did not raise enough money to build Maple Leaf Gardens in 1931, even with workers taking a pay cut. Smythe and his partners had to ask the workers to take a 20 per cent reduction in take-home pay, and take the difference in Gardens stock. Smythe gambled the future of the Gardens and his hockey franchise on the proposal, and it worked.

He was a military man through and through, and lived with the constant pain from a piece of shrapnel with which he was struck in the lower abdomen during the Second World War. But, next to the agony of losing his daughter in 1945, his greatest agony was watching the Leafs slip from family control. His son Stafford, along with millionaire John Bassett, lost a power struggle for the Leafs with Harold Ballard. After Ballard served his tax-evasion prison sentence in 1973, he ran the Leafs simply for the goal of making money, not to win. He regarded the team's history as an inconvenience, as it reminded fans that they deserved better.

When Smythe succumbed to a heart attack on November 18, 1980, his passing shook Toronto. "He was spit and polish, proper at all times," wrote famed Toronto columnist Paul Rimstead the day after Smythe's death. "Always in demand of perfection. Yet, underneath it all, this old geezer had a big heart and a definite sense of humour and fun."[1]

He died knowing his family no longer had a stake in the hockey team he had transformed into a dynasty. But, the fact that he managed to bring together the capital to build the Leafs, on a series of handshake deals and a few key winning wagers, is proof that Smythe would not be the man to try and beat at a game of Texas Hold 'Em.

The trophy awarded to the most valuable player of the National Hockey League playoffs is named in his honour. Despite the fact that he passed on decades ago, his name is still synonymous with Toronto hockey. Really, why would Conn Smythe need an elaborate memorial to commemorate his death, when he did so much in life?

How to Get There

To pay your respects to the great Conn Smythe, enter the cemetery through the main gates at Prince Edward Drive. Follow the main road straight ahead; don't be lured onto any of the side paths. When you get to the loop at the top of a ridge, look to your left. There will be three gravestones in a row in your line of sight; the Smythe family plot is the one to the left.

Park Lawn Cemetery is not only of interest to hockey fans because of Smythe, it is also where stars Corb Denneny and Harvey "Busher" Jackson are buried. Harold Ballard, the man who owned the Leafs through the turbulent years of the post-Smythe era, is also laid to rest here.

To locate graves, go to the office just inside the main gates facing onto Prince Edward Drive, and ask by name. Make sure not to use nicknames (ask for Harvey Jackson, not "Busher").

You can take the 501 streetcar west to the Humber Loop, then transfer onto the 76 Prince Edward bus, which goes by the cemetery gates. Or, take the subway to either Old Mill or Royal York subway stations. The north end of the cemetery borders Bloor Street between these stations. (See map on page 118.)

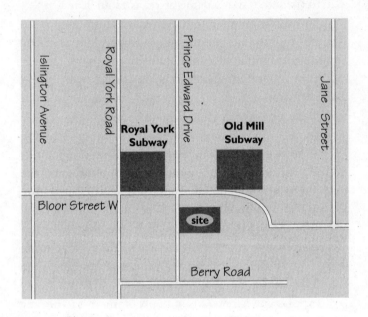

The Hockey Hall of Fame:
The Cup is in the Bank

By now, sports fans in North America are as used to the idea of the Hockey Hall of Fame being in Toronto as they are to Baseball's Hall being in Cooperstown, New York, or the Football Hall in Canton, Ohio.

But when you stop to think about it, Toronto is a rather odd choice for the Hockey Hall of Fame. While Atlantic Canadians and Montrealers may dispute the true birthplace of the game, one fact is for sure—the game was not born in Toronto. The city of Toronto did not win a

The Hockey Hall of Fame, still majestic at the corner of Front and Yonge streets. *S. Sandor*

Stanley Cup until 1914, 22 years after Lord Stanley first donated the trophy. Montreal and Ottawa won it many times before it got to Toronto.

Why is the Hall here? Out of necessity, really. When the concept of the Hall was first hatched, there was no home for it and no funds to build it. Throughout the '50s, the Hall's caretakers, spurred by Capt. James T. Sutherland, hoped to place a museum in Kingston, Ontario, Canada's first capital city. But, when no agreement on a home could be found, Conn Smythe, owner of the Maple Leafs, convinced the other five NHL owners to create a seed fund for a Hall of Fame. The Toronto cause was also aided by Sutherland's untimely death—when he passed, Kingston lost its largest booster.

With Smythe now behind the drive for a Hall, the location would be in his beloved hometown of Toronto. In 1961, with money donated from the Smythe-led NHL fund, the Hall of Fame opened on the Canadian National Exhibition fairgrounds. The Canadian Sports Hall of Fame had opened on the site two years before, but the original trustees of that Hall had agreed not to include hockey greats out of deference to the Hockey Hall's plans to go to Kingston.

The Hockey Hall of Fame held its official grand opening on August 26, 1961, with then-prime minister John Diefenbaker presiding, but the concept of a Hall of Fame had been around for a while. Smythe, Sutherland and a group of trustees had long been lobbying for a means to honour the greats of the game—and, in 1945, the first honoured members of the Hall were named. Until the location at the CNE was found, the Hall existed in name only, with more players and builders being inducted, but no place to showcase their accomplishments.

Statues line a mock hockey bench on the Front Street sidewalk. *S. Sandor*

The Hall lasted on the Exhibition site until 1993, when, under the leadership of chairman Scotty Morrison, the Hall was moved downtown, into the old Bank of Montreal building on the corner of Front and Yonge Streets. The branch, once the largest bank in Canada, was built in the 19th century and featured a 45-foot-high dome. It served as a head office for the Bank of Montreal until 1949 and was used as a branch for decades more. As a historic building, it would be preserved as part of the BCE Place development, a massive tower project that today acts as the headquarters for one of the Bank of Montreal's financial rivals, TD Canada Trust.

The restoration project brought the vault room, the focal point of the Hall of Fame, back to late-19th-century conditions, a must-visit for both the hockey fan and the fan of architecture.

The downtown site gave the Hall needed visibility;

aside from the late summer, when the CNE is in full swing, the Exhibition fairgrounds is a ghost town (save for special events such as the Molson Indy auto race every July), with no local traffic and all the charm of the abandoned amusement parks depicted in those great early episodes of *Scooby-Doo*.

The new Hall opened June 18, 1993, with the old bank serving as the Great Hall, the opulent centrepiece of the facility that houses the modern Stanley Cup and the major NHL trophies, such as the Hart Trophy (which goes to the league MVP) and the Conn Smythe Trophy (which goes to the MVP of the playoffs). The stained glass ceiling of the bank gives the Great Hall a truly holy feel. Glass plaques zig-zag through the Great Hall, bearing the portraits of hockey greats, coaches and builders who have been inducted.

There are some fascinating design details left from the Hall's former life as a bank. Maybe the most impressive are the panels depicting dragons protecting the money deposited in the bank from evil raiding eagles.

When you look up at the short biographies of the players inducted into the Hall, notice how there is no room for statistics. Yes, major statistical achievements are noted, but this is no place for a line-by-line statistical recap of a player's career. When you look at Wayne Douglas Gretzky's nameplate, you can't compare his annual totals as an Edmonton Oiler to his days as the captain of the Los Angeles Kings. You may know that Terrance Gordon Sawchuk's 103 shutouts is tops in NHL history, but you will be hard-pressed to tell in which season he put up the most zeroes.

In that way, the Hall of Fame is a great equalizer; once

a player is immortalized here, there isn't room for statistical debate. Was Joe Malone's 44 goals in 20 games back in 1917–18 a greater feat than Gretzky's 92 goals in an 80-game campaign? Here, the players' feats are reduced to a concise description of what they brought to the game, whether it be tenacity or artistry.

Noelle Der shows just how close fans can get to the Stanley Cup. Charles *C. Sandor*

In the old bank vault you will find the original Stanley Cup bowl, encased in glass. The original Cup is so brittle, it is not brought out of its case for fear it could crack. It was retired in 1969. As well, while each and every player's name is engraved on the Stanley Cup, the barrel has been filled. When the Cup has been filled with names, the trustees ensure that the top-most band on the barrel (the oldest) is gingerly removed from the Cup, with the other bands each moved up a notch (think of the barrel as an escalator moving up), with a new empty band added at the bottom, waiting to have the names of the next generation of champions engraved on it. The old, historic bands are then flattened and displayed in the vault, right by the vintage Stanley Cup, ensuring that the men who won the Cup decades ago will not be forgotten.

The current Stanley Cup is on display daily in the Great Hall. But how can that be? Surely, the podium on which the Cup sits should be empty when the Cup is awarded at the end of the NHL season, and on the days the winning players get to spend with it. How is it that if you pay your admission to the Hall, you are sure to see the Cup? Truth is, there are two in circulation; the "real" Cup is the one that is presented to the winning teams and spends time on the road with the players. When it is out of the hall, a very close, but not exact, replica is put in its place. Many of the misspellings of players' names on the original Cup are corrected on the replica.

The building itself is not without its mysteries. Legend has it, back in 1953 when the Bank of Montreal building was still in use as a bank branch, a teller by the name of Dorothy reported to work one morning, and proceeded to shoot herself in the offices of the bank manager. She and the manager were rumoured to have had an affair; when the manager decided to stick with his wife and end his romantic liaison with Dorothy, the teller decided to commit suicide in a spot where it would be very public, and very ugly.

Since the opening of the Hall, some say Dorothy's ghost still haunts the old Great Hall, and there have even been reports that she's made her way into the newer developments that surround the old Bank of Montreal building.

Outside of the Great Hall, the remainder of the Hall of Fame mazes through the new BCE Place development that surrounds it. In all, there are more than 50,000 square feet of exhibits and games. You can pick up a stick and fire a puck at a generated image of legendary goalie Ed Belfour. You can sit in a broadcast booth and try and call an NHL game shown in front of you on a video screen. And there are plenty of artifacts to see, from old jerseys, gloves and pads (make sure to check out the vintage goalie equipment; it really shows, more than anything else in the Hall, how much the game has changed over the years), game programs and photos.

Hockey films and videos are regularly shown at the Hartland Molson Theatre, located just inside the ticket gate at the Hall. The 128-seat theatre is also where the Hall plays host to all major media events, including press conferences for inductees.

How to Get There

Even though the old bank building that houses the Hockey Hall of Fame is right on the corner of Front and Yonge Streets, don't try to get into the building at street level. The entrance is one level below ground, facing onto a food court in the shopping-galleria basement of BCE Place. Toronto boasts a complex of interconnected shopping malls under its downtown office towers, and the Hall is part of this. These malls can be confusing to navigate; one wrong turn and you will feel like a mouse in a maze looking for a piece of cheese. In truth, there is something very Canadian about the Hall of Fame to our nation's great game being in a shopping mall, considering how much time Canadians spend huddled in malls, away from the elements.

To get there without getting lost in the shopping-mall maze, take the subway to Union and follow the signs for BCE Place/Hockey Hall of Fame.

Admission: As of 2006, adult admission to the Hall is $13, while youth admission is $9. That's a good value for an experience the hockey fan cannot miss. The Hall is only closed to the public for three days out of the year—Christmas Day, New Year's Day and Induction Day, when only VIPs and the new honoured members are allowed in to celebrate.

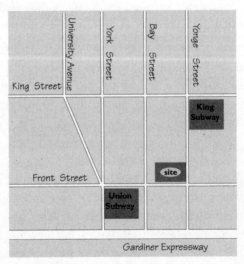

Thoroughly Historic, Thoroughly Modern: The Air Canada Centre

The Air Canada Centre is Toronto's modern hockey palace, a 665,000-square-foot structure seating 18,800 for hockey—and filled with every modern amenity a loyal fan or "one of the suits" in the corporate boxes could want.

But, when the designs for the new arena on the corner of Bay Street and Lake Shore Avenue were devised, hockey wasn't in the plans at all. The ACC was the pet project of the Toronto Raptors, the city's pro basketball franchise, who agreed to buy the site of the old Postal Delivery Building

The Air Canada Centre, facing York Street. *S. Sandor*

from the federal government in 1994. For four years, the project continued with the intent that the new arena to go on the site would be a basketball facility.

Meanwhile, the Toronto Maple Leafs were still looking for a new home to replace their old barn, Maple Leaf Gardens, which sat fewer than 16,000 for hockey and had the bare minimum of revenue-generating luxury boxes.

In 1998, the Leafs bought the Raptors. With the team came the Air Canada Centre project. Now, the arena would be a multi-purpose facility, which would house both hockey, basketball and, later, pro lacrosse in the form of the Toronto Rock. (With five championships in its first seven seasons, there is no doubt the Rock are ACC's most successful team to date.) Maple Leaf Sports and Entertainment spent $50 million on renovating a project that was still under construction in order to make the ACC more suited to hockey. But, considering the history of the site, changes to the building's design and purpose shouldn't have come as a major surprise. After all, the Postal Delivery Building had a history of multiple uses.

In 1938, the federal government decided better postal service was needed for the booming city of Toronto, and architect Charles Dolphin designed the Postal Delivery Building. Dolphin's design dressed up a boring mail-sorting warehouse with plenty of art deco flourish. The building featured bold lines, narrow windows and bas-reliefs of planes, delivery trucks and patriotic symbols that leapt at passersby from the grey exterior walls.

But, as the $2.25 million building was being built by Redfern Construction, the Second World War required a change of plans. The Department of National Defence appropriated the yet-to-be-finished building for use as an ordinance depot. When it was completed in 1941, there was no great grand opening; it was immediately put to use as part of the war effort. After the war ended, the DND gave the building back to the post office, and the building was finally used for the purpose for which it was originally intended.

When the Raptors bought the building it was long out of use, but it was protected as a historical site. So, the plans for the Air Canada Centre called for the preservation of much of the outer structure of the building. Today, two full wall facades have been saved, and 22 of the bas-relief carvings can be found on the walls. The most interesting spots are found in the Galleria, which is accessed via Union Station or off of Bay Street. This is a covered marketplace that uses the outer wall of the old Postal Building as part of its structure. Many of the wall fixtures of historical importance, including signage, have been moved to this wall, which can be viewed from the comfort of indoors.

Just outside the east doors of the Galleria, on the Bay Street side of the arena, is maybe the most interesting bas-relief of all: a rendering of natives going through a series of daily activities on a palm-covered South Pacific island. It would be hard to find a more bizarre piece of artwork on any of the other 29 NHL rinks. Walk through the Galleria to the west side of the building and you will find the steel spires, made to look like the rays of spotlights, of the public art piece "Search Light, Star Light, Spot Light," from noted sculptor John McEwen. It is listed as a must-see work of public art on the City of Toronto's ArtWalk tour.

Once you get inside the Air Canada Centre, though, it's hard to imagine that this was supposed to be a basketball facility. Yes, this is the home of the Raptors, but it is clear they play second fiddle to the Leafs. From the raf-

A stone relief by Gate 2 depicts a South Pacific island scene. *S. Sandor*

ters, there is but one banner celebrating NBA basketball. Meanwhile, 13 Stanley Cup banners, including the wins when the franchise was known as the Arenas and St. Pats, and 15 banners celebrating Leafs greats (Frank Mahovlich, Syl Apps, Charlie Conacher, Francis "King" Clancy, Walter "Turk" Broda, Irvine "Ace" Bailey, Bill Barilko, Johnny Bower, Tim Horton, Ted Kennedy, George Armstrong, Darryl Sittler, Borje Salming, Leonard "Red" Kelly and Clarence "Hap" Day) hang from the silver-grey roof girders. A "Memories & Dreams" banner celebrating the Leafs' final season at Maple Leaf Gardens and a "New Memories, New Dreams" banner celebrating the team's move to the Air Canada Centre makes that one purple Raptors banner seem insignificant.

Even the colour scheme of the seats is similar to the old Gardens, with the expensive lower-bowl seats sectioned off in platinum, gold and red (the gold and reds were the top-class seats in the old Gardens). The greens are the cheap seats, and the end seats are blue, just like they were in the Gardens.

A mural that rings the lower bowl features black and white images of fans dressed to the nines, clad in the fashions of the '50s, again a reminder of when the Gardens was the place to be, so much so that fans dressed to the nines for a Leafs game.

The Foster Hewitt Media Gondola, where the press sits six storeys above the ice, is named for the man who made history in the old gondola at Maple Leaf Gardens with his *Hockey Night in Canada* radio broadcasts.

Every little touch, each bit of art deco styling, was placed in the new building to make the culture shock as slight as possible for those who were so used to watching the Leafs at Maple Leaf Gardens. When the Leafs bought the Raptors, they knew they hadn't got themselves a new multi-purpose facility. What they got was a new hockey arena that could also be used in a pinch for basketball, lacrosse and concerts.

The $265 million building, costing more than 100 times more than the original post office building, opened on February 20, 1999, with the Leafs hosting the rival Montreal Canadiens. The fact that the Raptors used the building after the Leafs christened it is all the more proof that the ACC is seen as a hockey facility above all else. Leafs journeyman Todd Warriner got himself into the history books by scoring the first goal in the history of the ACC in the first period of play, but the accolades would be left for fan favourite Steve Thomas, who scored the overtime winner to give the Leafs a 3–2 win over their famous rivals.

In just its second hockey season, the Air Canada Centre hosted the NHL All-Star Game. As Toronto hosted the first-ever All-Star classic, the NHL decided that it would be appropriate for the 50th anniversary game to be held at the ACC. A sold-out throng of 19,300 saw the World Stars beat North American Stars by a 9–4 count. At the time, the All-Star Game format saw players divided not by division or conference, but by birthplace. Players born in North America faced players born in Europe. So, Leafs fans actually got to see their Swedish captain, Mats Sundin, facing down their goalie, Canadian Curtis Joseph.

Even though the game was held in Canada's largest city, it took on a decidedly Russian feel. Russian superstar Pavel Bure scored three times and added an assist and was named the Most Valuable Player. Two of his goals were set up by his kid brother, Valeri. In the third period, with the result well decided, fans embraced the Bures' display. Each time they hit the ice, the fans clapped in a traditionally Russian rhythm, as if they expected the Bures to break into a Barynya on the ice.

While Toronto fans are still desperately waiting for the Air Canada Centre to host a Stanley Cup final, it has hosted some other major hockey events. In 2004, the ACC was one of the host arenas for the World Cup of Hockey; included in those games was the final, which Canada won 3–2 over Finland. That game was significant not only because it represented a major international win for Canada, but it would represent the last time that NHL players would skate on Air Canada Centre ice before the lockout that wiped out the 2004–05 season.

The arena also hosted one of the two semifinal games, which Canada won 4–3 over the Czechs thanks to an overtime goal from Vincent Lecavalier. It was arguably the most exciting game played at the Air Canada Centre to date. Despite being outshot 40–24, Canada used strong goaltending from Roberto Luongo to get the game into overtime. In the extra frame, Ryan Smyth's no-look pass found Lecavalier in front of the Czech goal, and even though Lecavalier fumbled with the surprise pass, he still had enough time to settle it down and then fire it into the Czech goal. "I think our guys know they didn't play their best tonight and that they got through, even though they know maybe they shouldn't have," said Canada and Toronto Maple Leafs coach Pat Quinn after the game. "We were fortunate to survive."

ACC fans also got a treat in the preliminary rounds, when a Russian teenager named Alexander Ovechkin made his debut with his country's senior team in a 5–2 win over

The Galleria entrances celebrate the two main tenants: the Raptors and Maple Leafs.
S. Sandor

Slovakia. At just 18, the first-overall pick of the 2004 draft was the best player on the ice, and added a highlight-reel backhand goal. Even more memorable was the press scrum after the game. The Russian federation, using the normal road NHL dressing room, made the press wait 40 minutes before Ovechkin, whose English was poor at best, faced a crowd of more than 30 reporters and cameramen who refused to leave before getting an audience with Alexander the Great.

Maybe more memorable that night was an appearance by Micha Ovechkin, Alexander's dad, as the reporters waited for his mercurial son. "Am I proud of him? I am generally proud of him," said Micha, his words translated into English with the help of some Russian reporters. "He's a very special player."

Need Tickets?

Tickets are hard to find. Games are sold out well in advance, but there are plenty of scalpers to be found around the ACC who are more than willing to fleece you for a ticket. Unfortunately for most fans, this is the sole option for finding a seat. More depressing still is the fact that most of the corporate fans who take up the best seats in the house seem not to care that there's a game going on. Look down to the premium seats in the lower bowl at the start of a game—or at the start of a period—and they are mostly empty, as most of the premium ticket-holders are still enjoying snacks and beverages in the VIP area located under the bowl.

But here's a tip. NHL teams have to hold back some primo seats for the road team and guests for every home game. Because so many NHLers are from Ontario, and a game in Toronto is a big deal to which they invite many family and friends, most road teams use up the majority of their allocations for the games they have at the ACC. But, at a certain game-day deadline, the unused tickets are simply put up for sale. Tickets are available for between $42 and $385 (2005–06 prices) each. Try the game-day box office located in the Galleria, or ticketmaster.ca to see if you can rustle up any game-day released tickets.

How to Get There

Just get off the subway at Union Station and follow the signs. Walk south from the subway station through the GO Transit concourse at Union Station and you will see a tunnel that will lead you directly into the Galleria. No need to even put on a coat! If you prefer a more scenic route than offered by the subway, take the 510 streetcar to Union Station. It goes through Chinatown on Spadina Avenue and gives wonderful views of Toronto's Harbourfront area when it turns east on Queen's Quay heading towards Union Station.

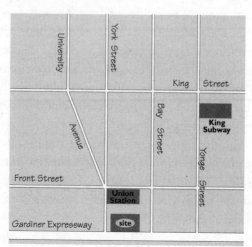

Ricoh Coliseum:
Roadrunners, Marlies and Empty Seats

Toronto is a hockey city unlike any other in Canada. Unlike other Canadian cities, Calgary or Vancouver, for example, where a junior team and an NHL team can draw huge crowds, Toronto fans focus the brunt of their attention solely on the big league.

Toronto has an unfortunate history of minor-league and junior teams that play to nearly empty houses and suffer from fan apathy.

The Toronto Marlies, the farm team of the Toronto Maple Leafs, made their debut in 2005, after Maple Leaf Sports and Entertainment decided that Toronto fans would flock to see the team's American Hockey League prospects in action before they made the big bold steps to the NHL. As well, moving the farm team to Toronto from faraway St. John's, Newfoundland, and Labrador would make it easier for the Leafs to call up players. A player could report to the big club in a matter of minutes.

So far, the experiment has been a big bust, with the Marlies playing to crowds well under half of the Ricoh Coliseum's 9,700-seat capacity.

But the Ricoh Coliseum itself is worth a look-see by serious hockey fans. The Coliseum, just like the Air Canada Centre, is a hockey arena built inside the shell of a great Toronto historic building.

The CNE Coliseum in 1928, before it was a hockey arena. *City of Toronto Archives, series 71, item 5749*

The Coliseum is located on the grounds of the Canadian National Exhibition, and is the result of a massive renovation/rebuilding of the old CNE Coliseum building, originally completed in 1921. The building, which cost around $2 million to build in 1921 (a massive budget back then), was called for by the CNE board as the centrepiece for a winter fair that would bring visitors to the grounds at a time of year when the Ex was deserted. The shell of the building was completed in time for a 1921 Royal Winter Fair, but because internal issues such as heating were not addressed in time, the planned 1921 Fair was cancelled. The building finally began hosting the Winter Fair in 1922, a role it has carried each and every November into the 21st century.

The Coliseum's most striking feature is the majestic arch, flanked by domed towers on the sides of the building.

In the late '90s, Lyle Abraham, owner of the Phoenix Roadrunners of the International Hockey League, moved his team out of Arizona as it could not compete with the NHL Coyotes, which had come to the desert from Winnipeg in 1996. He and the IHL looked to move the club to Toronto, and saw the old Coliseum as the perfect venue for a team.

By 2000, when the Coliseum/National Trade Centre was chosen as the host building for the big National Hockey League party around the All-Star Game, rumours circulated that the IHL was indeed interested in relocating a club to the Exhibition grounds. That party, which celebrated the first All-Star Game (played at Maple Leaf Gardens in 1947), saw bands and hosts dress in the garb of the Second World War era, with players, NHL execs and media dancing away to swing tunes at the old barn. The party also served to show off the possibilities of the old

Coliseum as a pro hockey rink; all the old brick building needed was a little bit of love.

In 2001, the IHL itself folded. But the dream to bring a new pro team to Toronto did not die—Abraham changed his business plan. Strong IHL clubs were going to the American Hockey League, the officially affiliated minor league of the NHL, and Abraham saw an opportunity. The Edmonton Oilers were struggling with their farm team, the Hamilton Bulldogs, which played to empty houses at Copps Coliseum, less than an hour's drive southwest on the Queen Elizabeth Way from the Ex. He made the Oilers an offer they couldn't refuse; he would pay the freight for their minor-league franchise, allowing the club to save money usually burned on the cash-losing business of player development.

The Oilers announced that the Roadrunners, their new farm club, would move to Toronto for the 2003–04 season, and CNE officials, happy to have the Coliseum rented out to a regular hockey tenant, undertook a $38 million renovation to the site to have it ready for the 2003–04 season. "When fans come here they'll see the beautiful old arches that were built in 1921," Roadrunners president Ernie Coetzee told the team's official magazine in 2003.[1] "They'll see the brick that was laid in 1921. That's been combined now with all the modern facilities of the sports and entertainment complex that will be an affordable alternative in today's marketplace."

The announcement infuriated the Toronto Maple Leafs. Not only did the Leafs not want competition from another pro hockey team from within the city limits, they did not want that team to have links to another NHL team. The Leafs protested when they found out the city would

The main entrance to the Coliseum, seen here in 2006, hasn't changed much from 1928.
S. Sandor

donate $10 million to the renovation project. The Leafs threatened to not agree to exhibition games in Edmonton, where throngs of old-school Leafs fans guaranteed nice home games in September for the Oilers.

But the Leafs didn't need to worry.

Despite the optimism of the Oilers, Abraham and Coetzee, the Roadrunners were a bust in Maple Leafs-mad Toronto. When the team debuted on Coliseum ice on November 1, 2003, after an extended season-opening eight game road trip to give renovation crews the time needed to finish the job, the Roadrunners were stumbling at two wins and six losses. That night, the Roadrunners entertained Buffalo's farm team, the Rochester Americans, and more than 9,500 fans came out for the occasion. A 1–1 tie saw future Buffalo Sabres star goalie Ryan Miller repel Roadrunners attack after Roadrunners attack.

But the crowds didn't stick with the team. For most nights during that AHL season, the arena was so empty, cold and quiet, that fans could hear the birds that had nested in the rafters of the brand-new roof, chirping as play went on.

The players were not household names in Toronto, either. Few Toronto sports fans, if any, could tell you a journeyman by the name of Jamie Wright, who played 124 career games with the Dallas Stars and Calgary Flames before joining the Oilers' organization, led the team in scoring with 55 points. Not many would remember the team barely scraped into the playoffs and was bounced in the first round.

By the end of the AHL season, the Roadrunners were missing rent payments. At the end of the campaign, the Oilers took over the Roadrunners and moved the team to Edmonton, in a ploy to replace the Oilers for the 2004–05 season that was expected to be lost to the NHL lockout. The team, renamed "Road Runners," was mothballed when NHL hockey came back in 2005–06.

But, the Oilers failure had turned into an opportunity for the Leafs. Now, the CNE had an empty arena it desperately wanted to fill. The Leafs now had access to a renovated building. Abraham and the Oilers had laid the groundwork, but failed in the business plan. Now, the Leafs could move their farm team into the Ricoh Coliseum.

As soon as the Oilers announced that their minor-league operation in Toronto was finished, the Leafs announced that its AHL team in St. John's would be moved to Ricoh Coliseum for 2005–06. The announcement that the St. John's Maple Leafs would be leaving Atlantic Canada would not come as a major surprise. In the decade that preceded the Leafs' move out of Newfoundland, Atlantic Canada had steadily been losing AHL teams. The Oilers' farm team in Cape Breton Island moved, as did the Montreal Canadiens farm team in Fredericton, New Brunswick, and the Calgary Flames AHL club in Saint John, New Brunswick. With all those teams gone, the Leafs were isolated in Newfoundland, with long road trips to Canada's eastern edge greeting teams from places as far away as Manitoba and the American midwest.

The St. John's Maple Leafs would be relabelled the Toronto Marlies, named for the famous junior team that used to call Maple Leaf Gardens home.

The Marlies debuted on Ricoh ice on October 12, 2005. Jean-Sebastien Aubin, who would finish the season with the Leafs, starred in goal, saving 29 of 31 shots as the Marlies beat the Syracuse Crunch 5–2. A promising crowd of 8,056 came out to the rink.

But hockey fans soon cooled to the Marlies, even though the team made the playoffs in its inaugural season and several of its players had successful stints with the parent Maple Leafs, including Aubin and defenceman Ian White. Soon, the Marlies were playing to crowds of fewer than 3,000, pretty well the same near-empty houses that the Roadrunners endured. Even playoff games drew poor crowds. The Marlies were eliminated from the playoffs by the Grand Rapids Griffins, the farm team of the Red Wings.

Despite the elimination, Marlies head coach Paul Maurice was promoted to the job as the bench boss of the Maple Leafs. Maurice, who led the Carolina Hurricanes to a six-game series win over the Maple Leafs in the 2002 Eastern Conference final, had been regarded as a major reason the Marlies, which did not boast the talent of its rival AHL teams, finished the season over .500 and made the playoffs.

The AHL's Philadelphia Phantoms are a success story; the team draws well, and the parent Flyers play just across the street. The Leafs can study from a successful model of having both parent and farm club playing in the same city. So far, the Leafs haven't been able to copy that success, and a game at Ricoh Coliseum does not yet stir hockey fans to make mass pilgrimages to the Exhibition grounds.

On January 28–29, 2007, Ricoh hosted the AHL All-Star Game and Skills Competition.

But, as long as the Leafs continue to operate the Marlies, the Ricoh's mix of old and new, much like the Air Canada Centre, makes it an attraction worth checking out at least once. However, judging by the fact bigger crowds come out for the Winter Fair and for concerts, Torontonians are not sold on the Ricoh as a hockey venue.

Need Tickets?

Tickets to Marlies games can be had for as little as $10. Go to the box office at Ricoh Coliseum the day of the game or call ahead at (416) 597–PUCK.

How to Get There

The subway goes nowhere near Exhibition Place, but there is a streetcar depot on the site, right across a pathway from the Ricoh doors. Both the 509 and 511 routes end at the Exhibition terminal. The 509 goes from Union Station, along Queen's Quay westbound, to the CNE. The 511 heads south down Bathurst Street from Bathurst station. (See map on page 144.)

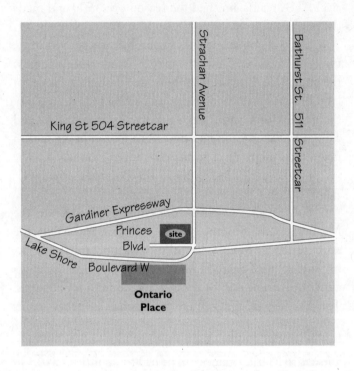

The Bar Exam & Trivia Tidbits

You're in Toronto on a Saturday night, and the thought of paying a scalper hundreds of dollars for a nosebleed seat at the Air Canada Centre makes you cringe. But you still want to watch the game in a great hockey atmosphere. Here's a guide to some of the best places in the city to catch the game.

Shakey's Original Bar and Grill
(2255 Bloor Street W, at Runnymede subway)

This famous west-end hockey watering hole was founded by former Leaf Mike "Shakey" Walton, who was arguably more famous for his party-hard ways than he was for winning Cups in '67 with the Leafs and in '72 with the Boston Bruins. Shakey also spent three years in the WHA with the Minnesota Fighting Saints, and there's no better place in Toronto for WHA memorabilia.

The walls are famous for their displays of paycheques issued to former Leaf players, so fans can appreciate just how cheap former owner Harold Ballard was to his staff!

Wayne Gretzky's
(99 Blue Jays Way)

This spot gets the No. 99 address, but you can spot it from

blocks away thanks to the giant, rotating rod-hockey figure on the top of the building. The food is your usual pub fare, but the real reason you're here is to see a whole museum's

A mock rod-hockey figure spins atop Wayne Gretzky's on Blue Jays Way. *S. Sandor photo*

worth of Gretzky memorabilia scattered throughout the bar and restaurant. There are Canada Cup jerseys and trophies and trinkets from the Great One's childhood years in Brantford, Ontario, but the best item in the whole place is the puck and stick used to break Gordie Howe's all-time points record. Really, it feels like an extension of the Hockey Hall of Fame.

Bottom Line Sports Bar and Grill
(22 Front Street W)

December 11, 1983. The New Jersey Devils beat a rebuilding Edmonton Oilers team by a 5–2 score. Wayne Cowley, who had bounced around the minors for more than a decade, gets into the Oilers goal after starter Bill Ranford is yanked due to injury less than three minutes into the game. It goes down as the only NHL game Cowley will ever play.

But Cowley, as the owner of the Bottom Line Sports Bar and Grill, stays close to the game. The bar boasts itself as the most upscale place to watch hockey in the city. Sure, there are nachos and wings to enjoy while watching the game on the big screen, but fans can also go for crab cakes or stuffed salmon. The Hockey Hall of Fame does a lot of promotions with the place, so it's got a solid stamp of approval.

Blue Goose
(1 Blue Goose Street, by Mimico GO station)

Located just a stone's throw from the Mimico Arena that the Shanahan family made famous through both their hockey and lacrosse exploits, the Blue Goose is a solid Leafs bar if the Buds aren't playing Brendan's New York

Rangers. As a Red Wing, Shanahan brought the Stanley Cup to the Goose, and the pictures on the wall will tell you all you need to know about how important he is to Mimico.

The Wheat Sheaf Tavern
(667 King Street W)

Opened in 1849, the Wheat Sheaf is one of the oldest establishments in the city. The walls display articles that celebrate the pub's history. Food and drink is basic pub fare, but the big screen TV has all the hockey action on game nights.

Elephant & Castle
(212 King Street W)

Part of the famous North American pub chain, the name may be decidedly English, but the atmosphere is as Canadian as can be on Leaf game nights. The King Street location is right at St. Andrew subway station and is only a couple of blocks from the Rogers Centre, and is a 10-minute walk from the Air Canada Centre. Can handle light snacks or a full-on meal for the hockey fan. There's a restaurant layout in front, with a full "office bar" in the back, featuring eight high-definition plasma screens. All Leafs games are show in high-definition on a seven-foot-wide screen.

Trivia Tidbits

What do Maple Leaf Gardens and the old Montreal Forum have in common? They were both closed out in similar fashion. How is that? Put it this way: goalie Jocelyn Thibault certainly has a thing for historic events. In 1996, Thibault was the winning goalie as the Montréal Canadiens beat the Dallas Stars in the last-ever game at the Montreal Forum. Three years later, as a member of the Chicago Blackhawks, Thibault got the win in the last-ever game played at Maple Leaf Gardens.

Now that's an impressive feat to brag about—being the winning goalie on the closing nights of both of Canada's old Original Six shrines!

The Chicago Blackhawks won the opening and closing games at Maple Leaf Gardens. But the Leafs do have something to hold over the Hawks. The Leafs won the last-ever regular season game at the old Chicago Stadium. On April 14, 1994, the Buds nipped the Hawks by a 6–4 count.

On October 14, 1947, Maple Leaf Gardens hosted the All-Star Game, with the NHL Stars defeating the Leafs by a 4–3 count. But the real story is the installation of glass on top of the boards, replacing the traditional wire fencing.

There is no doubt defenceman Al MacInnis is going to be

enshrined in the Hockey Hall of Fame. But, even though the man with the hardest slapshot of the '80s and '90s never played for the Leafs and isn't from Ontario, he's got an asterisk in the Maple Leafs' record book. On January 26, 1987, MacInnis bagged a hat trick as his Calgary Flames came back from a 5–0 deficit with just 15:28 left in the third period to beat the Leafs by a 6–5 score. At that time, it set an NHL record for the latest a team has been down by five goals and come back to win.

At the Air Canada Centre on November 29, 2000, the St. Louis Blues found themselves down 5–0 to the Leafs with just 15:27 left in the third before the comeback began. MacInnis scored in that comeback, as the Blues won 6–5 in overtime, breaking that Flames record by one second. Ironically, Alexander Khavanov, the Russian who scored the winner, would later go on to play for the Leafs.

The two greatest individual scoring games in the history of the NHL both involve the Toronto Maple Leafs franchise. On February 7, 1976, Maple Leaf Gardens was electrified when Darryl Sittler became the first player in NHL history to bag 10 points in a game, as he scoreed six times and added four assists in an 11–4 win over goalie Dave Reece and the Boston Bruins. Sittler was the second player in pro history to get a 10-point game, following only Jim Harrison, who got 10 points in an Alberta Oilers win over the New York Raiders in World Hockey Association action three years before Sittler's feat.

The Leafs franchise was also on the wrong end of a great individual scoring feat. Hall of Famer Joe Malone became the only man to score seven goals in a game, January 31, 1920. He scored every one of the goals on Toronto St. Pats netminder Ivan Mitchell.

The Toronto Maple Leafs aren't the only NHL team to call Maple Leaf Gardens its home arena. In 1950, the New York Rangers got to the Stanley Cup final, but were informed that they couldn't use Madison Square Garden because the circus had come to town. And the circus made a lot more money for MSG than NHL hockey. So, the Blueshirts had to use the Gardens as their home arena for the '50 final, which they lost to Detroit. In 1968, Maple Leaf Gardens hosted the Philadelphia Flyers as a home team. The Flyers used several NHL arenas for "home" games after a windstorm destroyed the roof of the Philadelphia Spectrum.

St. Mike's is Toronto's most famous junior franchise, but the Toronto Marlboros were more successful. The Marlies won their first of six Memorial Cups in 1929, when they defeated the Winnipeg Elmwood Millionaires.

Notes

The Granite Club

1. Henry C. Campbell, *Early Days on the Great Lakes: The Art of William Armstrong*. Toronto: McClelland and Stewart, 1971, pp. 28-29.
2. "Hockey," *The Globe*, Jan. 16, 1888, p. 2.
3. D. Rodwell Austin and Ted Barris, *Carved in Granite: 125 Years of Granite Club History*. Toronto: Macmillan, 1999, p. 115.
4. Ibid.

The Royal York

1. Andy Lyttle, "Leafs bleeding inwardly at their Preston clinic." *Toronto Star*, Apr. 7, 1938, p. 14.

Arena Gardens

1. "Canadiens won from Toronto Pros," *The Globe*, Dec. 26, 1912, p. 9.
2. "Stanley Cup Hockey did not make a hit," *The Globe*, March 16, 1914, p. 12.
3. "Vancouver helpless in deciding contest," *The Globe*, March 29, 1922, p. 10.

Ravina Gardens

1 Lou E. Marsh, "With Picks and Shovels," *Toronto Star*, Oct. 28, 1926, p. 13.

Varsity Stadium, Varsity Arena

1. Varsity Centre for Physical Activity and Health, www. varsitycentre.ca/.
2. R.Y. Cory, "Varsity 19, Laval 1," *The Varsity*, Jan. 23, 1908, Vol. XXVII, p. 224.
3. R.Y. Cory, "Sports," *The Varsity*, Jan. 2, 1908, Vol. XXVII, p. 173.
4. *UTS: 75 Years of Excellence*, Toronto: University of Toronto Press, 1985. p. 18.

Maple Leaf Gardens

1. Michael B. Vaughan and Judith Godfrey, *Proposed Designation of Maple Leaf Gardens under Part IV of the Ontario Heritage Act*, Ontario Ministry of Tourism, Culture and Recreation, Conservation Review Board, Toronto: Province of Ontario, 1990.
2. Tom Kerr, "Way cleared for Gardens to be named historic site," *Toronto Star*, Sept. 15, 1990.
3. Conn Smythe and Scott Young, *If You Can't Beat 'Em in the Alley*, Toronto: McClelland and Stewart, 1981, p. 112.

Lakeshore Lions Arena

1. Paul Waldie and Robert McLeod, "MLSE eyes campus site," *Globe and Mail*, Nov. 22, 2003, p. S4.

Here Lies Toronto's Greatest Gambler

1. Paul Rimstead, "The passing of a tough old legend," *Toronto Sun*, Nov. 19, 1980, p. 5.

Ricoh Coliseum

1. John Iaboni, "Majestic Facelift," *Toronto Roadrunners*, Nov. 1, 2003, p. 19.

Bibliography

"A History of the New York Rangers." New York Rangers Hockey Club website. 13 Jan. 2006. <http://www.newyorkrangers.com/tradition/history.asp>.

Austin, D. R., and Ted Barris. *Carved in Granite: 100 Years of Granite Club History*. Toronto: Macmillan Canada, 1999.

Bell, Scott. "Mutual Street Arena." Ballparks by Munsey & Suppes. 4 July 2003. 9 Jan. 2006. <http://hockey.ballparks.com/NHL/TorontoMapleLeafs/oldindex.htm>.

Burwash, Nathaniel. *The History of Victoria College*. Toronto: Victoria College Press, 1927.

Campbell, Henry C. *Early Days on the Great Lakes: the Art of William Armstrong*. Toronto: McClelland & Stewart, 1971.

Colombo, John Robert. *Haunted Toronto*. Toronto: Hounslow Press, 1996.

Cressman, Jim. "Knights Outrun Storm." *London Free Press*. 1 Dec. 2003.

Diamond, Dan, ed. *The Official National Hockey League Stanley Cup Centennial Book*. Toronto: McClelland & Stewart, 1992.

Durso, Joseph. *Madison Square Garden: 100 Years of History*. New York: Simon and Schuster, 1979.

Fancher, Diana. "Brilliant Hockey At West End Rink." *The Ledger and Recorder: the West Toronto Junction Historical Society Newsletter*. Summer 1996: 4.

"Farewell to a Hockey Shrine." *NHL This Week*. 8 Feb. 1999: 1+.

Filey, Mike. "Building History." *Toronto Roadrunners*. 1 Nov. 2003: pp. 14-16.

Friedland, Martin L. *The University of Toronto: a History*. Toronto: University of Toronto Press, 2002.

A Glimpse of Toronto's History: Opportunities for the Commemmoration of Lost Historic Sites. Toronto Historical Association. 2001.

"History of the Ontario Hockey Association: the Beginning of Our Game of Hockey." Ontario Hockey Association website. 15 Jan. 2006. <http://www.ohahockey.org/history.php>.

"History." Air Canada Centre website. 28 Feb. 2006. <http://www.theaircanadacentre.com/aboutACC.php?level=1&sectionID=4&parentID=164>.

Hockey's Heritage. Toronto: Hockey Hall of Fame, 1982.

Iaboni, John. "Majestic Facelift." *Toronto Roadrunners*. 1 Nov. 2003: 18+.

Lapp, Richard, and Alec Macaulay. *The Memorial Cup: Canada's National Junior Hockey Championship*. Madeira Park, B.C.: Harbour Publishing, 1997.

Mahovlich, Frank. Speech. Debates of the Senate (*Hansard*) 1st Session, 36th Parliament, Volume 137, Issue 116, Ottawa. 4 Mar. 1999.

"Marlies History." 2005. Toronto Marlies website. 12 Jan. 2006. <http://www.torontomarlies.com/history/marlies.asp>.

McKinley, Michael. *Etched in Ice: a Tribute to Hockey's Defining Moments*. Vancouver: Greystone, 1998.

"Mimico." *Toronto Neigbourhoods*. 1999. Maple Tree Publishing. 7 Jan. 2006. <http://www.torontoneighbourhoods.net/regions/etobicoke/81.html>.

Podnieks, Andrew. *Lord Stanley's Cup*. Bolton, Ont.: H.B. Fenn and Company Ltd., 2004.

Potts, J. Lyman. "Foster Hewitt." Dec. 1996. Canadian Communications Foundation website. 15 Jan. 2006. <http://www.broadcasting-history.ca/personalities/personalities.php?id=177>.

Reed, T.A. *The Blue and White*. Toronto: University of Toronto Press, 1944.

"Roy Conacher." 2001. Hockey Hall of Fame website. 20 Feb. 2006. <http://www.legendsofhockey.net:8080/LegendsOfHockey/jsp/LegendsMember.jsp?mem=P199801>.

Smythe, Conn, and Scott Young. *If You Can't Beat 'Em in the Alley*. Toronto: McClelland and Stewart, 1981.

Speers, Ian. "A Brief History of Varsity Arena." *Varsity Science & Technology*. 17 Mar. 1998. University of Toronto. 29 Mar. 2006.

Structures. Perf. Angus Skene. Videocassette. Rogers Television, 1998.

Vaughan, Michael B., and Judith Godfrey. *Proposed Designation of Maple Leaf Gardens Under Part IV of the Ontario Heritage Act*. Ontario Ministry of Tourism, Culture and Recreation, Conservation Review Board. Toronto: Province of Ontario, 1990.

Weiss, Bill, and Marshall Wright. "Team #39 1926 Toronto Maple Leafs (109–57)." Minor League Baseball website. 24 Feb. 2006. <http://www.minorleaguebaseball.com/app/milb/history/top100.jsp?idx=39>.

Wilkins, Charles. "Maple Leaf Gardens (and How It Got That Way)." *Maple Leaf Gardens: Memories and Dreams.* Toronto: Maple Leaf Sports and Entertainment, 1999. pp. 44–57.

Zweig, Eric. "Dawn of Hockey's Radio Days." *Ontario Hockey Now.* Apr. 2004.

Steven Sandor is the sports editor of *24 hours* in Toronto. He is the former editor-in-chief of Edmonton's *Vue Weekly* magazine, and the former North American editor of *Face Off*, a Europe-based hockey magazine. He is the former publications coordinator with the Edmonton Oilers Hockey Club. Steve has covered business, sports, politics and the arts for newspapers, magazines, television, radio and websites across Canada, the United States and Europe. He is a graduate of the Ryerson School of Journalism. His first book, *The Battle of Alberta: A Century of Hockey's Greatest Rivalry*, was published by Heritage House in 2005.

Steve supports the Arsenal Football Club, helped AC Misfits to a soccer title in Edmonton's rec league, and thinks that rock music is only good when played loud ... very loud.